The HOUSES of GREENWICH VILLAGE

by Kevin D. Murphy | Photography by Paul Rocheleau

ABRAMS, NEW YORK

Page 1: A group of former tenements in Grove Court, circa 1850.

Pages 2–3: "The Row" on Washington Square North.

Pages 4–5: Grove Street.

Page 6: The Church of the Ascension on Fifth Avenue and Tenth Street.

Page 7: West Ninth Street between Fifth and Sixth Avenues.

Page 8: "Twin Peaks," an apartment building cobbled together from two earlier houses by builder Clifford Reed Daily in 1925. Actress Mabel Normand reportedly celebrated its completion in 1926 by cracking a bottle of champagne over the roof.

Pages 10–11: A row of houses set exceptionally far back from the street allows for gardens at the front. In many parts of Greenwich Village, houses front directly onto the sidewalk.

Pages 12–13: Washington Square Park. To the right is the Washington Square Arch (1892), designed by architect Stanford White of McKim, Mead, and White.

Contents

Acknowledgments

The author would like to thank
the following for their part in
the creation of this book:

Kathleen Arffmann
Lemeau Arrott-Watt
Matthew Baird
Melissa Baldock
Andrew Berman
Richard Blodgett
Mosette Broderick
Ben Cherner
Sara Costello
Andrea Danese
Ronald V. DiDonno
Andrew Scott Dolkart
John Dougdale
Tim Forbes
Margaret Halsey Gardiner
Eric Himmel
Rev. Davis Given
Tom Harney
Anne Harrison
Eric Hughes
Christopher James
Anne Kennedy
Matt Larkin
Allison Ledes
Mitchell Lichtenstein
Peter Nadin
Ellen Nygaard
Richard Olsen
Emma O'Neill
Susan Packard
Andrew Paul
Howard and Katia Reed
Dale Rejtmar
Paul Rocheleau
Vincent Sanchez
Janice Sands
Jeffrey Scheuer
Ole and Sasha Slorer
Judith Stonehill
Laura Tam
Caroline and Nick Toms

"HE BELONGS TO THE FIRST RANK
OF SOLDIERS, NOT ONLY OF OUR
COUNTRY BUT OF THE WORLD"
U.S. GRANT

GENERAL PHILIP HENRY
SHERIDAN

Introduction

Nineteenth- and twentieth-century writers often remarked on the uncanny way in which the street pattern of Greenwich Village matched the neighborhood's character. Just as the Village resisted the uniform grid of streets and avenues that defined the rest of Manhattan, so the neighborhood's residents seemed to eschew many social conventions. With its ethnic diversity, vital gay and lesbian communities, and reputation for social and political radicalism, Greenwich Village appeared to many as a place apart from the rest of New York City, in which a tolerance for diversity has been made manifest in the patchwork of narrow streets and in the collection of houses representing the neighborhood's rich and varied history.

The traditional geographic definition of Greenwich Village considers it to extend from the Hudson River at the west, to Fourth Avenue and the Bowery at the east. Houston Street is customarily considered its southern boundary and Fourteenth Street and Union Square its northern one. In recent decades, however, the geographic definition of the Village has been stretched, to include a fairly large portion of the Lower East Side, sometimes referred to as the "East Village."

As Lower Manhattan and the Midtown area have both been developed with tall office buildings (to its south and north, respectively), Greenwich Village continues to offer relief from the scale of much of New York City. Townhouses were by definition human in scale, since they were not ordinarily served by elevators, and therefore limited to a number of stories that could be comfortably climbed. In contrast, apartment and office buildings piled up many stories to capitalize on valuable sites. In many parts of Manhattan, nineteenth-century townhouses were later replaced in great numbers by residential and commercial buildings that quite dwarfed their human inhabitants, whereas in Greenwich Village large swaths of the areas that had been built up with relatively small-scale houses in the mid-nineteenth century were preserved. (At one point in the twentieth century, Greenwich Village was even considered backward in relation to the rest of Manhattan because of its homey scale.)

The Village has largely escaped the incursions of high-rise buildings that have periodically threatened it since the early twentieth century. Its spatial oddities have thus been preserved. By the 1920s, the Village was known to contain odd cul-de-sacs and corners, the results of strange comings together of various street patterns, which provided insulation from the general hustle and bustle of the city. Patchin Place, for instance, a "quaint old neighborhood" of modest three-story brick houses located off Sixth Avenue was considered "a veritable cul-de-sac" apart from the rest of New York: "The isolation is complete. The hum and jarring noises of the city's traffic, the rumble of the nearby elevated trains. All those many discordant elements of city life are hushed to stillness in Patchin Place." The quiet of Patchin Place drew writers who were private, if not to say reclusive, including Djuna Barnes who allegedly shunned even such well-known visitors as the author Carson McCullers from Number Five, where Barnes lived from 1940 until her death in 1982. Across the alley, writer E. E. Cummings had moved into Number Four in 1923.[1] While not all of Greenwich Village can claim to be as detached from the rest of the city as Patchin Place, the neighborhood as a whole constitutes a leafy

A NOTE ON SOURCES
The introduction and essays on Greenwich Village houses are all followed by endnotes with specific historical references, and the text is followed by a selected bibliography that provides direction for further research in general histories of the neighborhood and period. In addition to these sources, the nomination to the New York City Landmarks Preservation Commission of the Greenwich Village Historic District, April 29, 1969, has served as an invaluable reference throughout. It can be consulted at the Web site of the Greenwich Village Society for Historic Preservation (http://www.gvshp.org/hdmaps.htm).

Life-size sculpture of General Philip Henry Sheridan (1831–88) in Christopher Park, Greenwich Village.

refuge of brick and brownstone townhouses much revered by New Yorkers and well known nationally—and even internationally— for the important role it has played in the city's and the nation's cultural life over the course of more than one hundred years.

If, on the one hand, the architectural fabric of Greenwich Village was especially hospitable to the countercultural groups that eventually made their homes there, on the other hand, the wood-frame and brick houses that dated from roughly the first three quarters of the nineteenth century (a period of enormous growth in the neighborhood), were adaptable

to a variety of uses. Originally constructed to accommodate extended families with moderate and slightly greater means who prospered from New York City's increasing economic activity after 1825, the rowhouses were readily divided into smaller apartments for the working class, or were converted to use as rooming houses, which provided a particularly important housing option for single workers as the Village declined in desirability after mid-century. The story of Greenwich Village, like the histories of other New York City neighborhoods, has, since its very beginning, been about cycles of rising and declining desirability. That story everywhere suffuses the histories of the individual houses that follow; together, they illustrate the history of Greenwich Village at the level of the individual dwelling.

Greenwich Village began its history as just that: a village. Until the early nineteenth century, "there was no more charming suburb of New York City than the sleepy village of Greenwich, looking from its tree-lined streets down over the western meadows to the beautiful Hudson and beyond to the shores of New Jersey." By the late eighteenth century, Greenwich was served by stagecoach service from the city located a couple of miles to the south, but still retained its essentially rural character. In 1731, Captain Peter Warren (later Vice Admiral Sir Peter Warren) had begun to assemble a parcel of three hundred acres of land between the present location of Broadway and the Hudson River to the west, and between the present Fourth Street to the south to the northern point where Twenty-first Street is now located. Later, Warren purchased an adjoining property bordered by Bleecker, Fourth, Perry, and Charles streets where James Henderson had built a fine house. By the early nineteenth century, the Warren house eventually passed into the hands of Abraham Van Nest and in 1865 was replaced by a row of brownstone houses. Yet during the early nineteenth century, the Van Nest Homestead was an important landmark in Greenwich Village and offered, according to comments made just prior to the mansion's demolition by General Prosper M. Wetmore, "a rare pleasure" of a well-preserved house surrounded by tranquil gardens: "No axe has ever invaded the sanctity of its groves. The mouldering trunks of trees that perished years ago still cast their shadows on the ground over which their youthful branches once answered with music to the breeze."[2]

The open landscape around the Van Nest house eventually succumbed to rowhouse development, as did most of the Village. In the antebellum period, Greenwich Village was swept up in the explosive development of New York City, which had begun in the late eighteenth century at the southern tip of Manhattan and moved northward. "By 1828 the streets had been paved and gaslit as far north as Thirteenth Street across most of the island," nearly coinciding with the northern boundary of Greenwich Village at Fourteenth Street. The Village, and indeed all of Manhattan south of Fourteenth Street, was exempt from the regularity that was imposed by the Commissioners' Plan of 1811. The basic element of that plan was the 200-by-800-foot block that was imposed over the landscape, creating what novelist Edith Wharton called "this cramped horizontal gridiron of a town."[3] The appeal of Greenwich Village, and of its houses, derives in great part from the neighborhood's being apart from the main grid of the city, which results in varied street patterns and in odd-shaped lots where they come together, providing unusual spaces for back gardens.

In addition to paved streets, Greenwich Village also possessed, by the late 1820s, an

A row of four houses in the Village, 1936. Photograph by Arnold Moses. Library of Congress, Prints and Photographs Division, Historic American Buildings Survey, Reproduction Number HABS NY,31-NEYO,37-1.

impressive public space: Washington Square, which has become the neighborhood's symbolic center. A portion of the property on which it is located was once a six-and-a-half-acre parcel of the so-called Herring Farm, which was sold at auction in 1797 to the city to serve as a potter's field, or burial place for the poor, in which capacity it served until 1825. Eventually, a gallows was erected on the site of the square as well, convenient to the cemetery. The location of such facilities at a remove from the city made a degree of sense, but within a couple of decades development began to move northward. The invention of Washington Square as a prestigious residential enclave, on the model of London's famous open squares ringed with attached townhouses, was the project of Philip Hone, a philanthropist, politician, and more. As a trustee of the Sailors' Snug Harbor, which owned twenty-one acres of land near what was then the potter's field, Hone was concerned with increasing the profitability of the group's real estate holdings, which he did by convincing the city to declare the cemetery the "Washington Military Parade Ground" (in 1826) and by leading the Common Council to enlarge it through an additional land acquisition. Soon after the boundaries of the new square were established, a row of Federal-style houses was constructed on its Fourth Street (south) side. The row of three-and-a-half-story, marble-fronted houses, with their identical elevations, emulated, like the square itself, the London model in which elite residential enclaves were established by open spaces surrounded by attached, or terrace, houses. The square itself was landscaped with turf and fenced, just as in the manner of the English residential squares.[4]

Following the completion of the houses along the south side and the landscaping of the square itself, other houses were built on the north side, Twenty Washington Square North having been the first in 1828–29 in the middle of the block west of Fifth Avenue. On the east side of the avenue, the famous Greek Revival row was built in 1832–33. Simultaneous with the construction of the row was the start of planning for a new facility to house the University of the City of New York, now New York University. Again emulating British models, the university's architects—the firm of Town, Davis & Dakin—modeled the building on the Collegiate Gothic style that was associated with the famous universities at Cambridge and Oxford. At great expense, the university completed the buildings by 1837. Just south of the NYU building, Minard Lafever designed the Reformed Dutch Church, which was similarly Gothic Revival in style and based on English prototypes. In the next decade, and continuing into the early 1850s, Italianate-style houses were built on the west side of the square, and additional residences filled in the other sides, thus completing the wall of buildings that bounded Washington Square Park. With fashionable private and public buildings, the park was the centerpiece of a prestigious residential district that extended outward from it, especially up Fifth Avenue to the north. The residents of the neighborhood included fairly prosperous extended families—of which the husbands and fathers commuted on the omnibus downtown to work—as well as their servants.[5]

The prestige that came from uniformity in house facades had an impact on building elsewhere in Greenwich Village where other terraces (or groups of rowhouses) rose as well. Perhaps one of the most celebrated was La Grange Terrace (Colonnade Row), designed and built by Seth Geer in 1833. A row of Corinthian columns stretched in front of the marble-faced houses, creating a monumental appearance that warranted high prices. While some clearly saw in La Grange Terrace a type of attached house that distinguished the domestic architecture of world capitals, others clearly found it foreign to American expectations. Critic Richard Grant White wrote of La Grange Terrace a half century after its completion: "A gloomier, more forbidding, more ridiculous structure for domestic purposes could hardly be found."[6]

While the early development of Washington Square Park and of terrace rows in other Greenwich Village locations drew

Street scene of houses fronting Greenwich Street, 1940. Photograph by Stanley P. Mixon. Library of Congress, Prints and Photographs Division, Historic American Buildings Survey, Reproduction Number HABS NY,31-NEYO,54H-1.

on an urban model that had originated in
European cities in the eighteenth century, its
later enhancement was part of the American
City Beautiful movement. That phenomenon was sparked by the Chicago World's
Columbian Exposition of 1893 for which a
"white city" was constructed on the shores
of Lake Michigan and consisted of a group of
glistening pavilions largely in a Neoclassical
style. The exposition sparked urban beau-
tification projects nationwide, aimed at
giving American cities the grandeur that was
popularly associated with European cities
such as Paris and Rome, where generations of
political and religious leaders had punctuated
the urban fabric with great monuments that
provided focus for grand avenues and impressive residential and commercial districts.

Thus, on the occasion of the celebration of the
centennial of President George Washington's
inauguration, in 1889 architect Stanford White
was commissioned to design a triumphal arch
(looking back stylistically to Roman imperial
triumphal arches and their nineteenth-century
imitations), which was erected across Fifth
Avenue, just north of Washington Square. Its
monumental style belied its transitory materials as well as the fact that it was designed
as a temporary structure through which a
parade was to pass. A more permanent ver-
sion was constructed within the confines of
the park itself, at the north side at the foot
of Fifth Avenue, and dedicated on May 4,
1895. At the laying of the cornerstone in 1890,
Henry G. Marquand, the chairman of the
Washington Arch Memorial Committee,

*View up Broadway toward
Grace Church, located on
the corner of Broadway and
10th Street. It was designed
by architect James Renwick
Jr. and consecrated in 1846.
Library of Congress, Prints
and Photographs Division,
Historic American Build-
ings Survey, Reproduction
Number HABS NY,31-
NEYO,67-2.*

remarked on the changing nature of New York's neighborhoods when he answered one critic of the project who had said that soon all of Greenwich Village would be consumed by tenements. Marquand argued that tenement dwellers were as susceptible to the perception of urban beauty as anyone else: "Happily there is no monopoly of the appreciation of things that are excellent any more than there is of fresh air, and in our mind's eye we can see many a family who cannot afford to spend ten cents to go to the park, taking great pleasure under the shadow of the Arch. This is the Arch of peace and good-will to men. It will bring the rich and the poor together in one common bond of patriotic feeling."[7]

By the time that the Washington Arch was completed, Greenwich Village was home to a wide variety of people, whose housing needs were addressed in different building types,

ranging from tenements to mansions. As the development of Manhattan had proceeded northward during the second half of the nineteenth century, some of the former residents of Greenwich Village (both white and African American) had followed. Newcomers included immigrant members of many ethnic groups, especially Italians. The conversion of single-family houses into rooming houses suited the incoming residents, including unmarried immigrants, as well as two other sometimes overlapping groups who, before World War I, had lent the Village its well-known character: bohemians and gays. Because of its celebrated hospitality to artists, intellectuals, and others who eschewed the bourgeois social norms of the period, Greenwich Village was felt to offer a relatively welcoming environment for lesbians and gay men. Added to that cultural attraction was the fact that the shift

A view from the northeast of the Church of St. John, 1934. Photograph by E. P. MacFarland. Library of Congress, Prints and Photographs Division, Historic American Buildings Survey, Reproduction Number HABS NY,31-NEYO,27-1.

in desirability for middle- and upper-class housing to the brownstone districts farther uptown had made the rooms, apartments, and houses of Greenwich Village relatively affordable for residents who were on the fringes of Manhattan's commercial economy.[8]

The following essays, focusing on houses dating from the early nineteenth century to the turn of the present one, represent the major stylistic developments in Greenwich Village's domestic architecture, and they illustrate the range of housing options that were available in the neighborhood. Some of the buildings represented here were constructed as relatively inexpensive rental housing, others were custom-built for wealthy families who sought to position themselves socially in New York City by occupying a mansion in a prestigious location in a fashionable neighborhood. More important, perhaps, the buildings were settings for a community that was mourned as houses were replaced by apartment buildings throughout Manhattan in the early twentieth century: "Family life may continue to be as pure and as strong in New York City as it ever has been. But to recreate that neighborhood instinct, which was once so characteristic of Washington Square and of Waverley Place, of Greenwich Village, of Chelsea and of Bloomingdale, will hardly be possible when the brown stone fronts have been replaced by seven- or eight-story apartment houses."[9]

In the mid-twentieth century, apartment buildings did encroach on Greenwich Village's traditional fabric, especially along Fifth Avenue just north of Washington Square where a number of nineteenth-century mansions were lost. The owners of the new apartment buildings appealed to "those who respond to the flavor and appeal of the 'Village' with its nearness to everywhere and everything," according to one advertisement. Indeed, the accessibility of Greenwich Village had been increased before World War I by the opening of the West Side subway and the extension of Seventh Avenue South below Greenwich Avenue, while the continuation of Sixth Avenue southward in the late 1920s had further contributed to making the neighborhood a viable place from which to

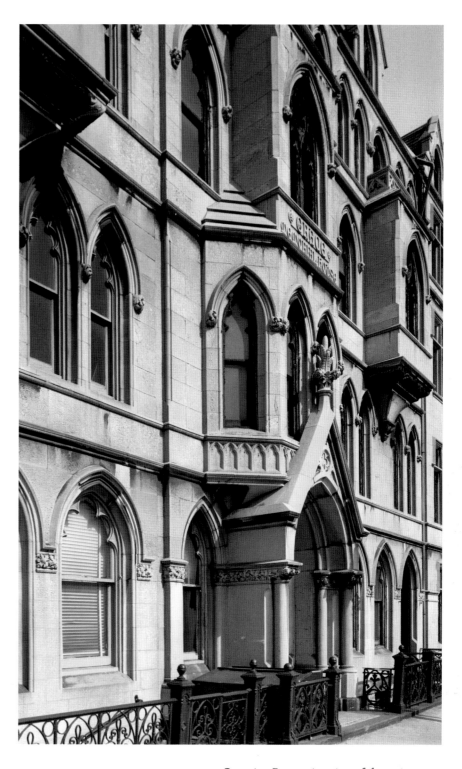

Opposite: Perspective view of the main elevation of 21 Stuyvesant Street. Library of Congress, Prints and Photographs Division, Historic American Buildings Survey, Reproduction Number HABS NY,31-NEYO,155-1.

Above: Perspective view of the main elevation of Grace Memorial House, designed by Renwick in 1883. Library of Congress, Prints and Photographs Division, Historic American Buildings Survey, Reproduction Number HABS NY,31-NEYO,68A-2.

132 West Fourth Street, 1936. Photograph by Murray Ezzes. Library of Congress, Prints and Photographs Division, Historic American Buildings Survey, Reproduction Number HABS NY,31-NEYO,38-1.

The New York Society Library. In 1855, the trustees of the New York Society Library selected Messrs. E. Thomas and Son as architects of their new building, which was nearly complete by 1856. Library of Congress, Prints and Photographs Division, Historic American Buildings Survey, Reproduction Number HABS NY,31-NEYO,15-1.

acommute to other parts of Manhattan.[10] As urban sociologist and journalist Jane Jacobs made clear in her pioneering study of 1961, *The Death and Life of Great American Cities*, Greenwich Village by mid-century was a vibrant and diverse community, the visual disorderliness of which had attracted some misguided attempts at "urban renewal." These were largely fended off, in part as a result of successful neighborhood efforts to limit the height and mass of new construction in Greenwich Village, which were codified in 1962 amendments to the 1916 zoning law.

The riot at the Stonewall Inn in 1969 catalyzed the national movement for gay rights, and drew new attention to Greenwich Village's diverse community. At the same moment, a widespread questioning of the postwar suburban ideal, which had dampened middle-class enthusiasm for urban living, sparked a new interest in the houses of Greenwich Village and inspired widespread renovation. While the architectural impact of this return to the city was positive—in terms of rehabilitated nineteenth-century buildings—it also had the somewhat less desirable consequence of pricing out of the neighborhood some of the very people who drew others to Greenwich Village: artists, intellectuals, and others who could not afford higher rents and escalated real estate prices. By 1971, one author could reflect on Greenwich Village that "Early in the century the Village was a flourishing artists' colony and acquired an aura of glamour and romance. The artists have long since fled, seeking less expensive neighborhoods, but the Village has desperately held onto its past reputation."[11]

More than thirty years have passed since the end of the Village's period as a bohemian enclave. The cost of buying or renting a residence in Greenwich Village has continued to increase as the neighborhood's historic houses, secluded settings, and quiet streets have drawn enthusiastic residents. Yet despite its gentrification and the influx of celebrity residents, Greenwich Village still provides, in its quiet backwaters and cul-de-sacs, spaces that have given birth to new countercultural movements that still inspire creative endeavors of all sorts to this very day.

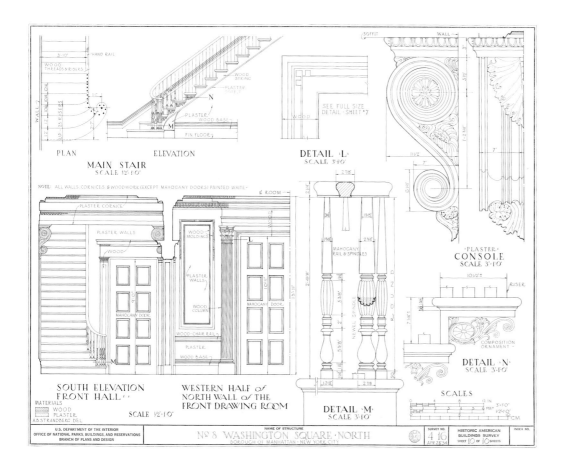

Drawing of architectural details at 8 Washington Square North. Library of Congress, Prints and Photographs Division, Historic American Buildings Survey, Survey Number HABS NY-4-16-C.

Drawing of front and rear elevations of 116 West Eleventh Street. Library of Congress, Prints and Photographs Division, Historic American Buildings Survey, Survey Number HABS NY-451.

Mantelpiece in the front drawing room at 8 Washington Square North, 1934. Photograph by E. P. MacFarland. Library of Congress, Prints and Photographs Division, Historic American Buildings Survey, Reproduction Number HABS NY,31-NEYO,18-5.

Interior of the front room (second floor) at 18 Greenwich Street, 1940. Photograph by Stanley P. Mixon. Library of Congress, Prints and Photographs Division, Historic American Buildings Survey, Reproduction Number HABS NY,31-NEYO,54G-5

Opposite: Main stairway and entrance hall at 8 Washington Square North, 1934. Photograph by E. P. MacFarland. Library of Congress, Prints and Photographs Division, Historic American Buildings Survey, Reproduction Number HABS NY,31-NEYO,18-3.

Doorway of rear parlor at 61 Washington Square North. Library of Congress, Prints and Photographs Division, Historic American Buildings Survey, Reproduction Number HABS NY,31-NEYO,37-7.

Opposite: Second floor of the reading room (looking south) at the New York Society Library, 1934. The reading room was the haunt of Greenwich Village writers such as Herman Melville and Willa Cather. The Library moved to new quarters on the Upper East Side in 1937, shortly after this photograph was taken. Photograph by E. P. MacFarland. Library of Congress, Prints and Photographs Division, Historic American Buildings Survey, Reproduction Number HABS NY,31-NEYO,15-3.

NOTES

1 "Patchin Place, Tenth Street, New York City," *American Architect* (Aug. 25, 1920): 250; Terry Miller, *Greenwich Village and How It Got That Way* (New York: Crown Publishers, 1990), 133–34.

2 R. W. G. Vail, "Unknown Views of Old New York," *New-York Historical Society Quarterly* (April 1959): 221–35.

3 Dell Upton, "Inventing the Metropolis: Civilization and Urbanity in Antebellum New York," *Art and the Empire City: New York, 1825–1861*, Catherine Hoover Voorsanger and John K. Howat, eds. (New York and New Haven: The Metropolitan Museum of Art and Yale University Press, 2000), 4–7.

4 Luther S. Harris, *Around Washington Square: An Illustrated History of Greenwich Village* (Baltimore and London: The Johns Hopkins University Press, 2003), 4–15.

5 Ibid, 16–31; Bayrd Still, "The Washington Square Neighborhood, 1830–1855," in *Greenwich Village: Culture and Counterculture*, Rick Beard and Leslie Cohen Berlowitz, eds. (New Brunswick, NJ: Rutgers University Press for the Museum of the City of New York, 1993), 111–19.

6 Upton, "Inventing the Metropolis," 15–16; Richard Grant White, "Old New York and Its Houses," *Century Illustrated Magazine* Vol. XXVI, no. 6 (Oct. 1883): 858.

7 Mindy Cantor, "Washington Arch and the Changing Neighborhood," in *Greenwich Village: Culture and Counterculture*, Beard and Berlowitz, eds., 83–86. Marquand's statement is found in *The History of the Washington Arch in Washington Square, New York* (New York: Ford and Garnett Publishers, 1896), 40.

8 Thomas Bender, "Washington Square in the Growing City," and George Chauncey, "Long-Haired Men and Short-Haired Women: Building a Gay World in the Heart of Bohemia," both in *Greenwich Village: Culture and Counterculture*, Beard and Berlowitz, eds.

9 "Apartment Life," *The Independent* (Jan. 9, 1902): 111.

10 Greenwich Village Historic District Nomination, April 29, 1969, Landmarks Preservation Commission LP-0489, p. 13; typescript courtesy of the Greenwich Village Society for Historic Preservation.

11 H. Dickson McKenna, *A House in the City: A Guide to Buying and Renovating Old Rowhouses* (New York: Van Nostrand Reinhold Co., 1971), 77.

Robert Blum House

1827 (renovated 1893)

As visual artists arrived in Greenwich Village at the end of the nineteenth century, to participate in the neighborhood's storied social and cultural life, its modest brick houses required adaptation to new uses. Former attics and spaces for boarders and servants gave way to garret studios, announced on the exteriors of the houses by expansive north-facing windows. Such was the case with this house, built in 1827 as one of a pair of nearly identical rowhouses erected by two masons, Henry Halsey and William Banks. In 1893 artist Robert Blum (1857–1903) hired the architectural firm of Carrère & Hastings—known for their design of the New York Public Library and of many ostentatious city and country residences—to transform the relatively modest house for his purposes. It became the stylish lair of a celebrated artist.

In the year that Blum undertook this project, he had recently returned from a three-year trip to Japan, where he was inspired to travel by an experience of his youth, much earlier, in his native Cincinnati. As he wrote in the first of several articles entitled "An Artist in Japan," Blum reported in *Scribner's Magazine* in April 1893, that two decades earlier, in 1872, he had attended a music festival in Ohio where "a boy was hawking ordinary Japanese fans. I think they were the first I had ever seen, and I became, what must have seemed to him, an amazing, if somewhat critical buyer. As enthusiastic a student, as I had been before an extravagant customer, I hung over the treasure, providently exploring my vast and fascinating prize." Having visited the "Japanese display" a few years later at the Centennial Exposition in Philadelphia in 1876, Blum became increasingly fascinated by Asia and eventually, as he reported, "I was on my way to Japan." Blum's interest in Japanese fans, and the country's

culture more generally, were not at all extraordinary for artists of his time; however, his embrace of "Japonisme" (the term used to describe Western artists' and others' embrace of Japanese visual culture in the nineteenth century) had a particular impact on the design and furnishing of his home and studio.

Blum's early artistic education had taken place at the Ohio Mechanics Institute, under the direction of the well-known painter Frank Duveneck, and later at the McMicken School of Design in Cincinnati. At the time of the Centennial, Blum was a student at the Pennsylvania Academy of the Fine Arts and a few years later, in 1879, he moved to New York City, where he found work as a magazine illustrator. However, Blum did not remain in New York for very long; the next year (1880) he went to Europe, meeting up with other former students of Duveneck's (the so-called "Duveneck Boys") and traveling as far as Venice, where he encountered James Abbott McNeill Whistler and became interested in printmaking. Blum's mania for collecting things Japanese, along with his fascination with prints, later motivated him to collect some six hundred ukiyo-e prints during his sojourn in Asia. Blum also shared with Whistler a commitment to producing works in pastel; indeed, Blum served as president of the Society of American Painters in Pastel and exhibited with the group around 1890.[1] In the mid-1890s, Blum's execution of a mural-painting project prompted *Scribner's Magazine* to comment (in January 1896) on the artist's incredible ambition, which had led him to yet another medium: "To one who has followed carefully Mr. Blum's career, its last development seems especially typical of a man who has risen with each opportunity; who, when he began his career as an illustrator, and with

View from the studio balcony to the window and skylight added in 1893.

hardly any artistic education [...] impatient and dissatisfied with his success as an illustrator, strove to become a painter."

Whistler's impact was felt in the United States in many areas of artistic culture; for example, in the revival of printmaking and the medium of pastel at the end of the nineteenth century. His influence on interior design was also substantial, especially as a consequence of the all-encompassing Japoniste aesthetic that was on view in the dining room he designed with Thomas Jeckyll for the house of Frederick Richards Leyland in London in 1876–77, the so-called Harmony in Blue and Gold: The Peacock Room (now installed in the Freer Gallery of Art in Washington, D.C.). A number of Japanese-themed rooms then appeared in New York mansions, for instance the "Japanese" parlor of William H. Vanderbilt.[2]

Blum's Japonisme was necessarily more restrained in his Greenwich Village house, which, even with the extension of the second story into the attic to create a double-height studio, still did not reach Vanderbilt proportions. Being active, at the time of the renovation, as a mural painter, Blum painted the walls of his first-story dining room with chrysanthemums, a familiar motif in Japanese art. Other rooms were decorated with fans and various forms that likewise bespoke Blum's familiarity with Japan. Near the time of his death, Blum even had a Japanese servant. After Blum died, the house was occupied by another artist, Jules Guerin (1866–1946), whose impact on it was not nearly as profound as his predecessor's. Guerin, a native of St. Louis, is perhaps best known for the renderings he did to illustrate the Chicago Plan of 1907. By 1908 Guerin had sold the house to Helen Olivia Phelps Stokes, a member of the prominent New York family whose members would own it through the 1980s. She was also a supporter of leftist political causes, as

were many Greenwich Village residents of her generation, and she was interested in the arts as well. For that reason, in the mid-1920s, Helen Stokes developed the back house on the property, which had probably originally been a rather utilitarian structure, into an Italian-inspired studio.[3] It was connected to the main house by a columned "loggia" and appropriately extended the exotic aesthetic of the residence—the result of Blum's earlier additions—to transform the entire property into the image of the Mediterranean world far from New York City.

Much of the character of the nineteenth- and twentieth-century alterations to the house, of historic interest because they represent the period of time in which Greenwich Village attracted cosmopolitan New York artists who saw their studios and homes as projections of their own artistic identities, are still intact. Recent renovations have been made in order to meet contemporary requirements, for instance the excavation of the basement level and the construction of a modern kitchen. Nonetheless, the artistic vision of Robert Blum is still intact.

NOTES
1 Julia Meech-Pekarik, "Early Collectors of Japanese Prints and the Metropolitan Museum of Art," *Metropolitan Museum Journal*, V. 17 (1984): 93, 103–4; Dianne H. Pilgrim, "The Revival of Pastels in Nineteenth-Century America: The Society of Painters in Pastel," *The American Art Journal*, Vol. 10, no. 2 (Nov. 1978): 43–62.
2 Marilyn Johnson, "The Artful Interior," in Doreen Bolger Burke et al., *In Pursuit of Beauty: Americans and the Aesthetic Movement* (exh. cat. New York: The Metropolitan Museum of Art and Rizzoli, 1986), 120–22.
3 Christopher Gray, *New York Streetscapes: Tales of Manhattan's Significant Buildings and Landmarks* (New York: Harry N. Abrams, Inc., 2003), 55–57; Daniel H. Burnham and Edward H. Bennett, *Plan of Chicago* (Chicago: Commercial Club, 1909); *Exhibition of Paintings of Jules Guerin of New York, Formerly of Chicago* (exh. cat., Art Institute of Chicago, March 1–21, 1906).

Opposite: Studio from its entrance way looking toward the north-facing studio window. Such windows were added to many earlier houses in the nineteenth century as the Village was increasingly home to artists and to those who wanted to be part of the art world.

Overleaf: The two fireplaces in the studio survive from an earlier period in the house's history when the space was divided into two rooms.

Dining room with a surviving portion of Robert Blum's murals preserved.

First-floor parlor with tiled mantelpiece. In the nineteenth century, the Tile Club was headquartered next door. The artwork on the ceiling is by the contemporary Austrian-born artist Otto Zitko.

Opposite: The bedroom is located in the rear portion of the house.

Above: Looking through the "loggia" (now enclosed with glass doors) toward the rear of the property.

Below: The modern kitchen was created by excavating the lower level of the house.

Thomas A. Wilmurt House

1827 (remodeled circa 1862)

This house, along with its neighbor, was built in 1827 by masons Henry Halsey and William Banks for their own use. The fact that this house was sold in 1862 to Thomas A. Wilmurt has led to speculation that it was substantially remodeled at that date in the then-prevalent Second Empire style, one hallmark of which is the French mansard-style roof, seen here with decorative iron cresting and arched dormer windows. Wilmurt's decision to purchase and renovate this house reflected the neighborhood's growing reputation among artists, writers, and intellectuals, for Wilmurt was a frame maker among whose clients was Tiffany & Co. The renovation of the house made what was by then a fairly old-fashioned building more stylistically up to date, and it also provided needed space for Wilmurt's family, which included his wife, Ann, and eight children.[1] Some of his children continued the family business, for in 1899 Thomas A. Wilmurt's Sons advertised picture frame "repairing and regilding done in the neatest manner."[2]

Wilmurt's Thirteenth Street establishment was important to the New York art scene at the end of the nineteenth century in that it served as agent for a number of institutions receiving works for exhibition, including the National Academy of Design, the Boston Art Club, and the Committee on Fine Arts of the State of New York for the World's Columbian Exposition in 1893. Wilmurt's high-class clientele brought trouble for the firm in 1883, however, when four of

twenty-seven paintings that Tiffany & Co. had sent to Wilmurt to be framed for one of its clients were stolen from Wilmurt's shop.[3]

The renovation for which Wilmurt was likely responsible not only added more space to the early house, but it also transformed that space in accordance with mid-century tastes. Most significant, at the parlor level, the two adjoining parlors—typical of the late Federal style—were combined into one large room, more on the scale of mid-century Italianate and Second Empire townhouses. Equally stylish marble mantelpieces and boldly scaled moldings were installed at the ceilings. At the rear of the parlor floor, the windows were extended down to the floor to become doors out to a porch overlooking the garden.

In 1909 the Wilmurt house was sold to Ferruccio Vitale, a landscape designer who was responsible for laying out the grounds of many expansive Long Island estates. He also redesigned the garden of this house and remained in residence until 1915 when it was purchased by James Graham Phelps Stokes, whose sister Helen Olivia Phelps Stokes, a labor activist, lived next door in the Robert Blum house. At that time the two houses were connected on each floor. James Stokes, who was from a prominent family but who had also prospered from substantial investments in railroads, was an active socialist politician. Through his political work he met Rose Pastor, a cigar worker and fellow socialist, whom he married in 1905, leading the

Adjoining gardens of the Robert Blum (left) and Thomas A. Wilmurt (right) houses. The loggia of the Blum house leads to a back building that provides additional living space while the more recent glass pavilion of the Wilmurt house is further back and to the right.

press to refer to her as "the Cinderella of the tenements." During their marriage Rose was active in the birth control movement and was even tried for antiwar activities in 1916. The couple divorced in 1925 and James married Lettice Sands a year later. After James Phelps Stokes died in 1960, his widow maintained both this house and the Blum house until the time of her death in 1988.[4]

The remarkable survival of the house's mid-nineteenth-century appearance is the result of its having been in the same family for most of the twentieth century. The current owners have updated certain portions of the house, notably the ground-floor kitchen, but have largely avoided making substantial alterations. Recently, they added a glass pavilion at the rear of the property, on the site of a dilapidated garden shed. Designed by architect Michael Haverland, who has taught at the Yale School of Architecture for ten years and who practices in the New York area, the pavilion gestures at once to the traditional greenhouse and to canonical modernist buildings such as Philip Johnson's Glass House of 1949 in New Canaan, Connecticut, and Ludwig Mies van der Rohe's Farnsworth House of 1951 in Plano, Illinois. Haverland writes that "this garden pavilion is the ultimate inside/outside space," in part because its front

wall—which provides a transparent visual connection with the garden and main house during cold weather—can be folded back in the summer to make it completely open to the outdoors. An open steel grid extends the lines of the pavilion's structure above its roof level—where a terrace was originally projected—to allow for a wisteria vine to create a green screen around the garden, which was designed by New York landscape designer Deborah Nevins. The strict geometry of the pavilion, seen across the garden, provides a focal point for the view from the house. As much as its aesthetic contrasts with that of the main building, the pavilion possesses a rectilinearity and austerity that harmonizes with the original late Federal style of the house.

NOTES
1 Gray, *New York Streetscapes*, 55.
2 "Picture Frames," *The New York Times* (Sept. 3, 1899).
3 "Four Stolen Pictures," *The New York Times* (Sept. 14, 1883); "Fine Arts for the Big Fair," *The New York Times* (Jan. 11, 1893); "National Academy of Design," *The New York Times* (Jan. 28, 1890).
4 Christine Stansell, *American Moderns: Bohemian New York and the Creation of a New Century* (New York: Metropolitan Books, 2000): 62; Gray, *New York Streetscapes*, 56.

Overlooking the garden is an oriel window, which was probably added in the 1860s since such elements were popularized by the contemporary Queen Anne movement.

View through the parlor toward the rear of the house with one of two marble mantelpieces to the right.

The second mantelpiece (1860s) in the parlor. The wide ceiling moldings were probably added at the same time.

Lengthened rear windows provide access to
the porch from the parlor.

The rear porch was likely an addition dating
to the 1860s.

The modernist back building with its front wall partly folded back. Wisteria vines have been planted and will eventually fill the metal grid that extends upward from the roof.

John Grindley House

1827

Architecture critic Ada Louise Huxtable described this house in her 1964 study, *Classic New York*, as being among "the best" examples of its type from the Federal period in the city. The Landmarks Preservation Commission considered this house and its twin neighbor as possibly "the two most important houses in age, richness of style, scale, and perfection of preservation" in the immediate neighborhood. As the Commission suggested, by the mid-1960s, many houses in the West Village had been demolished, subdivided, or substantially altered, whereas the Grindley house was preserved through its nearly continuous single-family use during the years in which other residences were being demolished to make way for industrial buildings in the immediate area, or cut up into smaller apartments.[1]

The history of the Grindley house mirrors the neighborhood's larger development from the site of country seats to a middle-class neighborhood of speculatively built houses to an enclave characterized by ethnic diversity. The neighborhood in which this house is located was originally part of the twenty-six-acre property that surrounded "Richmond Hill," a Georgian house built in 1767 for the British Major Abraham Mortier on land leased from Trinity Church. Later, the house was occupied by Sir John Temple, the first British ambassador to the newly formed United States, and it served as the residence of John and Abigail Adams (1789–90). Its most infamous eighteenth-century resident, and the originator of the concept of its urban development, was U.S. Senator Aaron Burr, who initiated plans to subdivide the land. The project was unrealized, however, at the time of Burr's duel with Alexander Hamilton in 1804 and subsequent arrest in New Orleans. It would take the entrepreneurial acumen of fur trader John Jacob Astor to bring about the development of the Richmond Hill property in the early 1820s. He had the actual residence relocated and transformed into a tavern, and cut down the bluff on which it had stood, overlooking the Hudson River, and plotted it out with sites for elegant townhouses like this one.[2]

Building this fine house was a speculative venture on Astor's part: soon after its completion it was sold to a shipping magnate named John V. Grindley.[3] Because of the neighborhood's proximity to the Hudson River waterfront, many homeowners with commercial interests in shipping and trade gravitated to the area in the early to mid-nineteenth century. Later in the century, as fashionable New Yorkers moved northward to new brownstone neighborhoods on the Upper East and Upper West sides, some of the by-then-disparaged neighborhoods of earlier townhouses were demolished or became derelict. Perhaps because of the architectural distinction of the Grindley house and its neighbors, its block attracted a number of fairly affluent Italian-American doctors. This house was owned by a Dr. Antonio Garbarino from 1930 until 1968. He enjoyed a loyal following among local residents who were drawn apparently as much by Dr. Garbarino's legendary concern for his patients as by the opportunity to see his fine townhouse in the course of office appointments.[4]

In addition to its exceptional interior detailing, the Grindley house possesses a characteristically (for the period) austere exterior enlivened by meticulously rendered decorative elements. As is typical of Federal-period urban architecture, the house has a

Grindley house facade.

View through the double parlors showing the exceptionally fine detail around the pocket doors and the ceiling.

flattish redbrick facade enlivened only by stone detailing at the windows, a cornice at the roof, and an entrance enframement. The latter, however, is quite elaborate. The door itself is framed by Ionic columns and half columns with sidelights between them. A wide transom above the front door lights the hallway beyond. The layout of the house is quite conventional, with a pair of parlors on the main floor, but the scale, detailing, and preservation of the house are quite exceptional.

NOTES

1 Landmarks Preservation Commission Report; August 16, 1966, Number 1, pp. 1–2; Ada Louise Huxtable, *Classic New York: Georgian Gentility to Greek Elegance* (Garden City, NY: Doubleday, 1964).

2 From an unpublished history of the neighborhood by Richard Blodgett to which the author kindly directed me.

3 Roland S. Pisano, "Living with Antiques: American Art in a New York City Townhouse," *The Magazine Antiques*, Vol. 156 (Nov. 2000): 734–43.

4 As recounted by Richard Blodgett in his history of the house.

The lyre-back dining chairs and serving table in the back parlor, now a dining room, are nineteenth-century New York pieces.

The hallway is painted to simulate stone
construction; the paintings and furnishings
are nineteenth-century American.

The dining room sideboard was made in
New York, circa 1815–25. The painting is
a nineteenth-century American still-life.

*Second-floor sitting room with its stone mantelpiece,
nineteenth-century French furnishings, and a
collection of nineteenth-century American paintings.*

Bedroom with stone mantelpiece and nineteenth-century New York and New England furnishings.

Cornelius Oakley House

1828

In the 1930s, the Index of American Design (an effort of the Federal Arts Project to identify the highlights of American fine and decorative arts) cited this house as one of the finest examples of the late Federal style in New York City. While the aesthetic characteristics of the house are consistent with the most fashionable urban dwellings of the late 1820s, the history of its occupants and use illustrates the transition of Greenwich Village from an enclave of merchants to a neighborhood known for its communities of artists and intellectuals.

Oakley built his house on a lot that was owned by one of the largest property holders in Lower Manhattan: Trinity Church, which owned land throughout the neighborhood. Oakley was a partner in the mercantile firm of R. & C. Oakley on Front Street in Lower Manhattan. His decision to build a house uptown, removed from the activity generated by the port and waterfront on the southern tip of Manhattan, was typical of prosperous merchants of the 1820s and 1830s who were willing to travel from their homes to their places of business on a daily basis (something that would not have been necessary in previous decades when prestigious residential areas were located near the port) in order to have large, elegant homes in the latest architectural styles. Moreover, by moving to more exclusive residential neighborhoods, merchants insulated themselves from "the helter-skelter residential mix of the downtown colonial city" in which city dwellers of various economic and social levels had lived and worked side by side.[1] The construction of the house may not have been just a personal choice, but was possibly also a speculative investment, as Oakley appears to have been living on West Fourth Street by 1845. Charles Oakley, likely Cornelius's brother, owned an adjoining property and leased it to his son-in-law and business partner, Edward Roome, who built a house similar to this one in 1835–36 and then sold it for a profit shortly thereafter. The neighborhood thus offered attractive living quarters, as well as opportunities to profit from real estate investment, to merchants with capital in the 1820s and 1830s.

The Oakley house exemplifies the transition between the Federal style and the Greek Revival style that prevailed by the early to mid-1830s, the latter represented by the houses of "The Row" on the north side of Washington Square. Whereas those houses of a slightly later date have doorways framed by disengaged columns, standing out from the facade as fully sculptural elements, here the entranceway is flanked by Ionic columns, but they are drawn back into the facade of the brick building. Beside the columns are half-length sidelights (characteristic of the Federal style), and against the walls are engaged columns. The columns visually support the large fanlight above, a feature that Henry James associated in his novel *Washington Square* (1880) with the Federal style, which he saw as having been thoroughly outmoded by the Greek Revival in the 1830s.

Other aspects of the house would have been considered out-of-date by the 1830s. The materials used are brick and marble, both familiar from the colonial houses farther downtown. In addition, the house is three-and-a-half stories

Oakley house facade (at right) with an adjoining house of a slightly later date to the left.

The fanlight above the outside front door is echoed by a similar element on the inside entrance. Typical of rowhouses throughout the nineteenth century, the two doors created a small vestibule that offered some amount of privacy when visitors came calling.

Opposite: Double parlors separated by pocket doors and framed by Ionic columns, a treatment likely inspired by contemporary published builders' guides.

high with a steeply pitched roof punctuated by three dormers. The roof profile, prevalent during the eighteenth and early nineteenth centuries, was considered unfashionable later in the nineteenth century when other means of treating the attic story of a rowhouse had been developed. For example, in some Greek Revival examples, a half wall at the attic level was masked by a wide classical cornice punctuated by windows and surmounted by a shallow-pitched roof. A low roof, nearly invisible from street level, was thought to be more classical in feeling, while tall dormered roofs were considered almost medieval.

The interior of the house was consistent with earlier urban houses in that it had two principal rooms on each floor. In scale, however, the house was larger than Federalist examples, and certain of the details at the doorways and fireplaces betrayed the emergence of the Greek Revival idiom.

In 1920, the underlying land was sold by Trinity Church to a real-estate investment company. Like many Greenwich Village houses, this one had been converted to apartments after the neighborhood's social cache had faded in the twentieth century. In the 1970s, however, as the renown of Greenwich Village as a desirable residential neighborhood spread, the house was purchased by an owner sensitive to its historic character who reversed some of the earlier alterations (including removing a stair that had been installed through the ceiling of the rear parlor on the main level) and carefully maintained the remaining historic features of the principal spaces. In the place conventionally occupied by a tearoom addition, a new kitchen was constructed.

In recent decades, the top floor of the house has been converted into a veritable nineteenth-century artist's garret by photographer John Dougdale. Using a large-format camera, and techniques that date back to the nineteenth century, Dougdale has produced images that echo the qualities of historic pictures, but that also embody contemporary sensibilities. The aesthetic he brings to his photography is the same one he has applied to the construction of his studio and living quarters in the attic story of the Oakley house, and some of the things found in his

studio appear in his pictures. Dougdale has opened the roof of the attic with skylights, created a modern kitchen fully in keeping with his old-fashioned sensibility, and decorated his studio with extraordinarily beautiful nineteenth-century objects. Dougdale's taste runs to the sorts of things that were extremely popular in the antebellum period, such as the copper-luster pitchers and other ceramic objects that he groups around his studio. At the rear, overlooking the garden, he has built a narrow sleeping porch, which seems an ideal lookout onto the Village. For Dougdale, there is no separating his photographic art from the art that is the creation of his working and living space in the Oakley house. As with the most interesting art produced in Greenwich Village, Dougdale's is not merely *made* in the Village, but is inspired by and deeply connected with the fabric of the community itself.

NOTES

1 Daniel J. Walkowitz, "Artisans and Builders of Nineteenth-Century New York: The Case of the 1834 Stonecutters' Riot," Rick Beard and Leslie Cohen Belowitz, eds., *Greenwich Village: Culture and Counterculture* (New Brunswick, NJ: Museum of the City of New York and Rutgers University Press, 1993), 209.

The hanging to the left of the fireplace in the parlor emphasizes the extraordinary scale of the house. The ceilings are about ten feet high.

In the parlor, an antique Windsor chair is combined with a nineteenth-century French table as well as Continental and Asian decorative objects.

Above: The enclosed sleeping porch off of John Dougdale's studio overlooks the rear garden.

Opposite: Like many Greenwich Village attics, this one has been transformed into an artist's studio with the addition of a skylight.

The attic-level studio with
Dougdale's large-format camera,
a nineteenth-century antique; his
photos on the wall; and a variety of
nineteenth-century furnishings. To
the right is a "fancy" painted settee.

William Depew House

1830

Within two decades of the date of this house's construction, its vernacular Federal style could already be considered nostalgically by *Putnam's Monthly*. An article entitled "New York Daguerreotyped," which appeared in the March 1854 issue, philosophized that "New-York is continually rising like a phoenix from the ashes, and, at each revival with increased elegance and splendor. The old economical style of buildings, without a shadow of ornament, which succeeded the more imposing structures of ante-revolutionary times have nearly all disappeared, and scarcely a vestige of old New-York remains." In recent decades, the author noted, "Plain brick fronts have been succeeded by dressed freestone and sculptured marble; plate glass has become universal and lace window drapery has displaced the old chintz curtains which once flaunted their bright colors through small window panes." Speaking of the use of Greek Revival forms in townhouse design around 1830, in place of the earlier style, *Putnam's* commented that "The introduction of pure Greek models into England and this country, produced some slight improvement on this plain brick style." This house, although built at the moment at which Greek-inspired forms began to transform the appearances of Greenwich Village buildings, nonetheless clings to an older idiom that prevailed between the end of the Revolution and the late 1820s. Generally referred to as the Federal style, it was part of a larger revival of interest in the material culture of Roman antiquity, inspired by excavation and publication of the ruins of ancient Rome.

Although this house is faced with brick, it is similar to a familiar townhouse type that proliferated in New York and other cities,

examples of which were built with wood-frame construction. It is two-and-a-half-stories in height with dormers in its steeply pitched roof. Soon after 1830, such roof profiles would be considered old-fashioned. The name of the architect is not recorded, perhaps because the house was based not on a specially commissioned set of plans, but instead on published designs, or carpenter's guides, that proliferated in the period and that offered suggestions for the designs of urban houses. Among the most prolific guidebook authors was Asher Benjamin (1773–1845), a Connecticut-born architect (or "housewright") whose first book, *The Country Builder's Assistant,* was published in Greenfield, Massachusetts, in 1797. Among Benjamin's later books was *The American Builder's Companion* (1827), which contained plans and elevations for townhouses in the Federal style. Benjamin's books were especially useful for the doorway details they provided, including drawings of columns and other neoclassical elements.[1] The most elegant features of the Depew house facade are the Doric columns that frame the entrance and the transom that surmounts it. The treatment of the doorway is particularly Federal in period and contrasts with later Greek Revival houses, which were typically framed by nearly freestanding columns.

Not only was this house built at a time of stylistic transformation in Greenwich Village architecture, it also rose at a moment when New York City was becoming an increasingly important national and international commercial center, as a consequence of the completion of the Erie Canal in 1825 (among other factors). The builder of this and the adjacent house, William Depew, was a grain measurer and

Depew house facade with simple engaged Doric columns framing the front door with a brownstone stoop and belt, which course above the English basement.

View from the stairhall to the parlor at the rear of the first floor.

Opposite: Rear parlor and front stairhall. A ship's portrait hangs above a late eighteenth-century demi-lune table.

likely profited from increasing trade in New York City in the 1820s. Evidently, the construction of the two houses was a speculative undertaking since Depew sold the house to David S. Brown, a tallow chandler (or candle maker), before it had even been finished. In 1830, candles were still the principal source of light, just prior to the development of various kinds of oil lamps for illuminating domestic and other spaces. Thus Brown may well have been engaged in a profitable business that generated cash for real-estate investment or speculation.

In plan, the house follows a familiar format, with a side hall providing access to two major rooms at each floor. The double parlors are connected by an open archway, creating a sense of spaciousness at the main level. As is customary in rowhouses of the period, the ceiling heights and elaborateness of finishes decrease as one moves upward in the house, indicating a hierarchy of internal spaces. Like many other houses in Greenwich Village, this one was also expanded at the rear by a tearoom addition, in this case in 1921. Recent renovations by the present owners have further extended usable space, with the development of the basement as a modern kitchen, the conversion of a shed into a guest room at the rear of the first story, and the conversion of cramped attic rooms into children's bedrooms and a playroom.

With the adjoining house, this property represents one way in which Greenwich Village's lots were developed in the nineteenth century. Between the two houses is a "horsewalk," or passageway (now closed by iron doors), that led to the rear of the property. There, it has been speculated, was a shop that could be accessed without passing through either one of the houses. Thus the rear of the property was made available for productive use. On their upper stories, the two houses share the space above the horsewalk, which extends the floor areas in the modestly scaled buildings.

NOTES
1 Jack Quinan, "Asher Benjamin and American Architecture," Introduction to a special issue of the *Journal of the Society of Architectural Historians*, Vol. 38, no. 3 (Oct. 1979): 244–53.

View from the front to the rear parlor.

Rear parlor fireplace flanked by glass-fronted cabinets and a pair of French armchairs.

Front parlor with its fireplace. The mantelpiece was likely originally supported at each side by a column.

Bedroom with its original wide-plank pine floors refinished. Pine floors were originally intended to be painted or covered with fitted carpet.

A guest room replaced a shed to the rear of the first floor.

Above: Stairs descending to the kitchen.

*Opposite: The exposed beams in the kitchen are
part of the original structure.*

Merchant's House Museum

(Seabury Tredwell House), 1831–32

This house, located at 29 East Fourth Street, was built on speculation around 1831 by a hatter named Joseph Brewster and was purchased a short time later, in 1835, by a merchant named Seabury Tredwell. The house opened to the public as a museum in 1936 and represents an extraordinary survival that includes the furnishings associated with Tredwell's daughter Gertrude who lived there until age ninety-three, in 1933. On the other hand, its original setting is mostly lost, the house being almost the last survivor of a row that once gave the block a nearly uniform appearance. As Robert Fuller, writing in *The New York Times*, commented at the time the house opened as a museum, "Quite different from the neighborhood of loft buildings, garages, and warehouses one finds today was the glittering vicinity into which Seabury Tredwell moved his family in the spring of 1836," when high society was moving northward from Lower Manhattan.[1] Nevertheless, the house preserves in many respects the type of domestic environment to which a prosperous merchant could have aspired in the early nineteenth century.

The Merchant's house represents the transition from the Federal to Greek Revival styles that took place in the 1830s. In plan, the house is much like its predecessors in Manhattan and other cities. It has a side hall plan, like earlier houses, and two major rooms on each floor. The major rooms are at the level above the English basement and the house has two magnificent parlors joined by an archway framed with columns that reflect the Greek Revival. Among the most outstanding features of the interior are the gasoliers in the two parlors, which date to around 1870. The Manhattan Gas Company, incor-

porated in 1830, would have made gas available to the Tredwell house as early as 1835.[2] Elaborate plaster ceiling medallions are found in each parlor. The kitchen is located at the rear of the ground level and the dining room at the front. A pair of bedrooms, joined by a closet with fitted drawers and compartments, occupies most of the floor above the parlor level. A small room that may have originally been used as an office is located above the front entrance. Like many other townhouses of the period, the parlor level was extended by a tearoom of wood-frame construction.

Like earlier houses in the Georgian and Federal styles, the Merchant's house is constructed of red brick enlivened with white stone and painted-wood details. The doorway is framed with fully disengaged Ionic columns, indicative of the Greek Revival style. The steep roof and dormers are holdovers from earlier periods and would soon become outmoded features as flatter roofs came to be preferred. Both the interior and exterior details are refined and are comparable to those published by Minard Lafever (1798–1854) in his books *The Young Builder's General Instructor* (1829), *The Modern Builder's Guide* (1833), and *The Beauties of Modern Architecture* (1835). Built about a decade later, the house of Tredwell's cousin, the Skidmore house (1844–45), another survivor of the nineteenth-century streetscape, represents the complete assimilation of the Greek Revival aesthetic into domestic architecture with its bold entrance columns.

Three of Tredwell's daughters remained in the house for some seventy years. When Sarah Kissam Tredwell died in 1906 *The New York Times* reported that "The employees of the hat and feather manufacturers of East

Opposite and right: The double parlors on the main floor. The circa 1870 gasoliers were restored in 2007, and they hang from elaborate plaster ceiling medallions.

*The bed in the rear chamber on the second floor
is hung with nineteenth-century printed textiles.*

At the basement level, the kitchen looks out onto the garden. The wide hearth is fitted with a nineteenth-century cast-iron stove. Other nineteenth-century cooking implements are also on display.

View from the rear parlor on the first floor. The tearoom addition is visible to the right, just outside the window.

Fourth Street, just west of the Bowery, poked their heads out of their windows yesterday and commented on the fact that there was a crape on the door bell of the old-fashioned dwelling No. 29." When the reporter went to investigate, "A woman who answered the bell said the sisters had lived a simple life ever since the death of their parents, and had always been opposed to leaving the old home, although all the other old families of New York had moved uptown. They had been the neighbors of the Astors, the Van Cortlandts, the Potters, and others." At the time of her death, Sarah Kissam Tredwell was claimed to have left an estate, largely comprising New York City real estate, valued at more than six million dollars.[3]

Sarah's sister Gertrude Ellsworth Tredwell strenuously denied this estimation of the family's wealth in a letter to the newspaper's editor ten days later, where she wrote, "I beg to insert this paragraph to contradict and absolutely deny the erroneous statements set forth in the columns of the daily *Times* of Saturday last respecting the surviving daughters of the late Seabury Tredwell. Suffice it to say, despite the assertions made to the contrary, they are only in comfortable circumstances, and are practical, thoroughly good loyal citizens of the substantial old type of character handed down from generations back . . . "[4] After the death of Gertrude Tredwell, the architectural reputation of the Merchant's house grew, especially as ever more of the early nineteenth-century fabric of New York City has been lost.

NOTES

1 Robert N. Fuller, "A Landmark and Museum," *The New York Times* (May 3, 1936).
2 Mimi Sherman, "A Look at Nineteenth-Century Lighting: Lighting Devices from the Merchant's House Museum," *APT Bulletin*, Vol. 31, no. 1 (2000): 37–43.
3 "Vanderbilts' Relative Dies in Old Fourth St.," *The New York Times* (Oct. 13, 1906).
4 Letter to the Editor of *The New York Times* signed "G. Ellsworth," *The New York Times* (Oct. 24, 1906).

Opposite: The axial design of the twentieth-century garden is emphasized by paving.

Malcolm McGregor House

1832

Its perfectly preserved basket-shaped urns at the stoop, topped with pineapples, have made this house a landmark in Greenwich Village as an outstanding example of a late Federal townhouse. In similarly original condition are the Ionic columns framing the doorway. These features suggest an increasing interest in the Greek Revival among New York house builders during the early 1830s. While the size and two-and-a-half-story height of the house are consistent with the Federal style, the dormers also retain their original detailing, notably the pilasters that flank the windows. As much as it is architecturally significant, however, the house is also important as the home of an artistic Greenwich Village couple in the early twentieth century.

A section view of the house published in a home-design magazine in the 1950s illustrated the adaptability of the nineteenth-century interior to modern use. At the center of each floor, paneled double doors can be used to close off a small space. On the main level, that space contains a butler's pantry that makes it possible to use the rear room, overlooking the garden, as a dining room. In the 1950s, the ground-level front room (the customary location of a family dining room) was referred to as a breakfast room. On the second story, the double doors that closed off the dressing room at the center of the house could be opened to join the bedroom and sitting room at that level as one space.

At the time that the house was profiled, it was the residence of "a pair of modern artists": painter-portraitist Saul Schary and his wife, who designed and produced a line of textiles under the name Hope Skillman. The house functioned as a showcase for her upholstery

and drapery fabrics; Schary's paintings hung "in nearly every room." Schary (1904–1978) was born in Newark, New Jersey, and educated at the Art Students League in New York, at the Pennsylvania Academy of the Fine Arts in Philadelphia, and in Paris. He was a friend of the painter Arshile Gorky, among other artists, exhibited widely in the United States, and was among those painters shown at the gallery of Charles Daniel, which focused on the work of American and European modernists between 1913 and 1931. Schary's modernist works received better critical reception than his more traditional canvases. A notice of a New York exhibition of Schary's work, published in *Parnassus* in 1931, declared that the artist "paints fine, small tempera abstractions and large, bad figure pieces." While the magazine was skeptical of a few of his "awful, academic canvases," it conceded that with only a few exceptions "Schary's work was all worth a careful seeing" and praised a large abstract oil, "admirably held together by color and composition."[1] In addition to his following as a painter, Schary was also known as an illustrator and printmaker.

Hope Skillman Schary (ca. 1908–1981) was a graduate of Goucher College and began her career as an editor of *Parnassus* and other magazines, which is likely how she met her husband. She was something of a rarity in her day by virtue of owning and operating a textile manufacturing firm that focused on cotton fabric, both for household use and in women's clothing, the latter making her widely known in the fashion industry. She had worked for two different textile manufacturers before starting her own business, Hope Skillman, Inc., in 1942, which she

McGregor house facade with its basket-shaped, openwork iron urns topped with pineapples at the stoop.

ran until the 1960s when she retired. Hope Skillman Schary took leadership roles in the textile industry as well as in women's organizations, including the National Council of Women of the United States of which she was a two-term president in the 1970s.[2]

Although by the 1950s, when the Scharys were in residence in this house, many critics decried the loss of Greenwich Village's authentic bohemia of the first couple of decades of the twentieth century, nevertheless, as this couple's attachment to the neighborhood demonstrates, it still attracted cultural producers in some number. William Barrett summarized the somewhat contradictory character of the neighborhood in the 1950s when he wrote that "Most of what the Village once stood for is gone and will never return. What remains is either middle-class or desperate, without charm or prinked up for tourists. Yet, there is an informality, a charm, and an odd human warmth about this neighborhood that makes one prefer it to other parts of Manhattan."[3] Despite subsequent change and gentrification, Greenwich Village continues to call forth an identity that is unlike those of other prestigious New York City residential neighborhoods.

Like many Greenwich Village properties, this one offered enough depth to allow for an additional building at the rear of the garden. In place, perhaps, of an earlier outbuilding, a later owner (likely the Scharys) erected a separate studio building. Positioned against the rear wall of the property, the studio faces roughly north and has double glass doors and skylights to capture the optimal lighting for an artist. More recently, the yard has been excavated to open up the rear of the house, paved with stone, and planted to visually connect the main building and the studio. The green oasis between the house and the studio was probably very important to the Scharys (who also owned a country house) since, as Hope Skillman Schary wrote in an article on rural American art colonies published in *Parnassus* in 1933, "[T]he art colony does act as a necessary balance to the hectic city winter; it provides for the relaxing of codes, physical and spiritual, encourages expansion of contacts and ideals, and establishes the artist in a place that is his own."[4] Schary implied, although she did not say as much, that the true birthplace of "a real American school" (of which she was a great champion) was in New York City, and in particular in Greenwich Village.

NOTES

1 "Federal Period Piece," *House & Garden*, Vol. 89 (April 1946): 73–75; "Recent and Current Exhibitions in New York," *Parnassus*, Vol. 3, no. 2 (Feb. 1931): 14; Julie Mellby, "Letters from Charles Daniel to Peter Blume," *Archives of American Art Journal* Vol. 33, no. 1 (1993): 13–26. Schary's personal papers are in the collection of the Archives of American Art, Washington, D.C. (reels 1007 and 1049).

2 Walter H. Waggoner, Obituary, *The New York Times* (May 28, 1981): 21.

3 William Barrett, "Greenwich Village: New Designs in Bohemia," in *The Empire City: A Treasury of New York*, Alexander Klein, ed. (New York and Toronto: Rinehart & Co., 1955), 104–5.

4 Hope Christie Skillman, "The Suburban Side," *Parnassus*, Vol. 5, no. 5 (Oct., 1933): 27.

Entrance hall with a small vestibule at the front door.

Front parlor where the original fireplace is flanked by built-in bookcases.

A corner of the front parlor in the McGregor
house, now the home of a writer.

View from the front parlor toward the rear
of the house. The space between the front
and rear parlors, which can be shut off with
pocket doors, has been fitted with a bar and
refrigerator and other conveniences since the
kitchen is on the lower level.

Bedroom with tiled fireplace surround and a Greek Revival mantelpiece in keeping with the house's aesthetic.

View from the kitchen toward the studio at rear.

Kitchen on the lower level with glass doors leading to the rear yard.

Saul Alley House

1833

This house is one of a group built on property owned by the Sailors' Snug Harbor, a retirement home for seamen that had received a bequest from Captain Robert Randall of a large farm. The first occupant of the house was Saul Alley, a Quaker from Providence, Rhode Island, who was a merchant, like many well-off residents of the Washington Square neighborhood. The house was built, however, by John Johnston, who also built the adjoining house at Number Seven. By constructing a large house in the up-to-date Greek Revival style, Johnston appealed to well-off Manhattanites who were following the development of prestigious residential quarters northward from the site of the first settlement on the southern tip of the island.

Johnston was a Scot who had immigrated to the United States in 1804. He was a partner in the import-export firm of Boorman & Johnston with James Boorman who would reside at Thirteen Washington Square North. (Boorman and Johnston both contributed to the mercantile character of the Washington Square neighborhood.) Johnston's granddaughter, Emily Johnston de Forest, recalled that when her grandfather and his associates built the block of houses on the north side of Washington Square, it "was then so far uptown that it was, for all practical purposes, in the country." Building on unimproved land gave Johnston and his collaborators the opportunity to construct particularly large houses. Numbers One through Six Washington Square North, at about twenty-seven feet in width, are substantially wider than most Manhattan rowhouses, and Number Seven (Johnston's own residence) is more than thirty feet wide. Despite differences in scale between the houses, Johnston's

involvement in their construction (including Number Six) meant that several residences on the block shared certain elements on the interior. Emily Johnston de Forest recalled that her grandfather had used his merchant connections to purchase furnishings and architectural elements in Europe and elsewhere; for instance, Johnston reportedly bought marble mantelpieces in Leghorn, Italy, for both his own and the Alley house.

The layouts of the interiors were virtually identical, with a parlor at the front of the main floor and a drawing room at the rear, separated by mahogany doors framed with columns, and with a piazza providing access to the garden at the rear. Emily Johnston de Forest remembered that her family ordinarily dined in the front room at the basement level, but that "whenever my grandmother gave a formal 'dinner-party' or a 'coffee-drinking' it was always in the drawing room."[1] Another author recalled that the front basement level was used more flexibly, serving as a "joint nursery, breakfast, family room," with "its large windows looking out on the areaway." Typically, the parlor level was entered from a vestibule at the top of the stoop, which led to an "arched reception hall, beyond which was a long corridor which ran back under the stairs," rising back to front to the upper level where there were two principal chambers, or bedrooms. Servants' quarters were located even higher up in the house.[2]

To some extent the grandiosity of the houses on Washington Square North was determined by the original ground leases from Sailors' Snug Harbor in 1831. Those documents called for the lessees to construct a "good and substantial dwelling house, of the width of said lot, three or more stories high, in brick

Alley house facade, part of the Greek Revival row on Washington Square North.

or stone, covered with slate or metal." The houses were "to be finished in such style as may be approved of by the lessor." Evidently, the officials of the Sailors' Snug Harbor were amenable to the Greek Revival style, which was expressed in the classicizing details of the entranceways framed by pilasters and columns. To ensure the desirable residential character of the neighborhood, the leases also prohibited the construction of outbuildings at the rear of the property that would have accommodated noxious industries such as smith shops, forges, nail factories, and others.[3] The carriage houses that were allowed on the back lots of the Washington Square houses were subsequently converted to artists' studios and residences. In some instances, carriage houses or stables for the houses at Washington Square North had been erected on the opposite (north) side of the broad alley at the rear of the properties, subsequently known as Washington Mews, thus leaving the entire backyards of those houses open.

Johnston lived in Number Seven until his death in 1851, after which time it was owned by his widow until she died at age ninety-seven in 1873. During her latter years, Mrs. Saul Alley was among the elderly women who gave the block its name: Widows' Row. Number Six passed out of the Alley family in 1869, when it was owned by the family of Sabina E. Redmond, who remained there until 1912. Subsequent long-term owners, Mr. and Mrs. John R. Morron, owned the house from just after World War I until the death of John Morron in 1950. An account of the house, written at the time of Morron's death, described Six Washington Square North as "the only

house of the entire Row, east as well as west (of Fifth Avenue), that was still in its perfect, original condition, and beautifully maintained." By the mid-twentieth century, the character of the neighborhood had changed entirely from its earlier status as an enclave of wealthy merchants, and the grand merchant houses had declined in desirability as the apartment house became the new standard of Manhattan luxury. Indeed, in 1939 Numbers Seven through Thirteen Washington Square North were converted into the facade of a much larger apartment building that rises behind them, leaving only a small portion of the original houses to hold the wall along the north side of the square. On the opposite (west) side of Fifth Avenue, Numbers Fourteen to Eighteen Washington Square North were lost to an apartment tower at 2 Fifth Avenue in 1951–52.[4] However, as nineteenth-century historical revival styles were rescued from the critical disdain in which they were held during the reign of high modernism at mid-century, and as townhouses returned to desirability, the remaining houses around Washington Square were highly valued once more, although now many are owned and occupied by institutions (New York University, in particular) rather than by the families that originally filled them.

NOTES
1 Emily Johnston de Forest, "History of Washington Square New York" [c. 1930], Historic American Buildings Survey #4-16-B, Library of Congress.
2 Ann Kees, "Washington Square North," *The Magazine Antiques* (Mar. 1945): 163.
3 Lockwood, *Bricks and Brownstone*, 84-85.
4 Ibid, 84-85.

Main staircase leading from the entrance to the second floor. The high level of detail in the house is indicated by the brackets below the second-floor landing.

Marble mantelpiece with a nineteenth-century corner chair.

The passageway between the drawing room and parlor is framed by Ionic columns, in keeping with the house's Greek Revival style.

The fireplace is flanked by Ionic columns echoing details found elsewhere in the room. The mid- to late-nineteenth-century clock is an interpretation of an earlier (late eighteenth or early nineteenth century) tall case clock form.

Black marble fireplace in the dining room surmounted by a nineteenth-century gilt mirror.

David Christie House

1834

James Fenimore Cooper, in his *Notions of the Americans: Picked Up by a Travelling Bachelor*, written in 1825 and published in 1828, could well have been describing a house such as the David Christie house when he wrote:

> There is a species of second-rate, genteel houses, that abound in New York and into which I have looked when passing with the utmost pleasure. They have, as usual, a story that is half sunk into the earth, receiving light from the area, and two floors above. The tenants of these are chiefly merchants, or professional men, in modest circumstances, who pay rents of from $300 to $500 a year. You know that no American who is at all comfortable in life will share his dwelling with another. Each has his own roof and his own little yard. These buildings are finished, and exceedingly well finished, too, to the attics containing on average six rooms, besides offices and servants' apartments.

Reading Fenimore Cooper's description a quarter century later, architectural critic Montgomery Schuyler marveled at how the escalation of New York real estate prices had put the middle-class house out of reach for many: "If it [the house of Fenimore Cooper's time] be no longer eligible, that is because the price of land over all the surface of Manhattan Island, if not throughout the whole city of New York, has appreciated that to make a comfortable house, with the limits of a basement, two stories, and an attic would be a piece of extravagance."[1]

Although it was built about a decade after Fenimore Cooper published his description of the common middle-class New York house, this example follows the earlier pattern very closely. It has two stories above the English basement, and a steeply pitched dormered roof, encompassing six major rooms, per the author's description. In its detailing as well, the house is very much of the earlier Federal period, for the wood and stone elements that contrast with the brick walls are very delicate in comparison to the more sculptural features of the later Greek Revival style. The one suggestion of the popularity of classical Greek architecture in New York in the 1830s are the columns that flank the front door.

The oval was a commonly used form in Federal-style architecture and decorative arts, and here it appears on the left side of the facade, above the entrance to a walkway that leads to the back of the property. In Greenwich Village, the appearance of diagonal and even winding streets in some locations had produced some exceptionally deep or oddly shaped pieces of land. In some of those situations, the rear part of the property was developed for a stable, office, or an entirely separate residence or "back house." Some of these buildings were nearly as large and solidly constructed as the main house, while others were more shoddily constructed tenements that catered to the large numbers of immigrants and other lower-income people who sought housing in an increasingly expensive market. In some cases the back house was an existing building, dating perhaps to a time when the Village was more rural in character and the houses set farther from the street, but more often they were constructed after the building at the front of the property. In this instance, the back house is a substantial, brick, multistory building. Back houses were also accessed by a variety of means, in some cases through the front building, but here a walkway provides a degree of privacy for both dwellings.

Columned entrance with oval panel to the left.

Christie house facade, part of a streetscape of buildings of various scales and dates.

The neoclassical architecture in the front parlor provides a backdrop to a pair of Barcelona chairs and other modernist furnishings.

The construction of the main house coincided with a period of intensive residential construction following the completion of the Erie Canal in the mid-1820s that brought increased commercial activity to New York City and drew new residents. The city's population nearly doubled between the 1820s and 1840s, from 124,000 in 1820, to 203,000 in 1830, to more than 300,000 ten years later. As a result, New York experienced a residential building boom during the 1820s and 1830s.[2] From the early 1820s, merchants and then artisans increasingly sought out residences at a remove from their places of work on the waterfront, on the southern end of the island of Manhattan. Speculative builders responded to and fueled this movement by building houses of varying sizes "near the western side of the island and up its center at the advancing urban edge, near Washington Square" and elsewhere in Greenwich Village.[3] The extensive building, however, did not satisfy the growing need for housing, brought about by the influx of new residents during the mid-nineteenth century.

When new middle- and upper-class neighborhoods were developed farther north in Manhattan during the second half of the nineteenth century, and Greenwich Village declined in desirability, this house, along with thousands of others, was converted from a single-family residence to a multi-apartment building. The attic story was made into a separate living unit accessed through the main stair hall. An early twentieth-century kitchen with vintage appliances survives as evidence of this period of multifamily use. Elsewhere, the house reflects the careful renovation by the current owner who returned it to single-family use and filled it with a combination of mid-century modern and historic furnishings that perfectly complement its refined Federalist architecture.

NOTES
1 Montgomery Schuyler, "The Small City House in New York," *Architectural Record* Vol. VII, no. 4 (April–June, 1899): 357–58.
2 Lockwood, *Bricks and Brownstone*, 6.
3 Dell Upton, "Inventing the Metropolis: Civilization and Urbanity in Antebellum New York," in Catherine Hoover Voorsanger and John K. Howat, eds., *Art and the Empire City: New York, 1825–1861* (New Haven Yale University Press, 2000), 16.

An original fireplace flanked by bookcases.

Sitting area at the rear of the parlor level.

View from the sitting area at rear looking toward the front parlor. A more open floor plan was created on the first floor.

In the kitchen, the red brick foundation walls are left exposed.

The owner's collection of wood planes and other nineteenth-century implements and ceramics.

The attic-level bedroom was once part of a rental apartment.

Southwestern-style attic bedroom. An old mantelpiece functions as the bed's headboard.

Edward S. Innes House

1842

This house was one of three adjoining residences constructed by a cigar maker named Edward S. Innes. Evidently, Innes's intention was not to live in the house but rather to rent it out or to resell it, taking advantage of the great demand for housing in Manhattan in the 1840s. The construction of these houses for Innes was also an indication of the growing prosperity of the cigar-making industry in the city: *Illustrated New York: The Metropolis of To-Day* observed in 1888 that "From comparatively inconsiderable proportions the cigar industry has grown to vast magnitude in New York during the past quarter of a century." Savvy enough to get involved in the emerging cigar industry, Innes also spotted a contemporary increase in demand for housing (and consequently, in the prices charged for rentals) and entered the real estate market with these three houses. Although the later history of Greenwich Village brought changes to the houses, a contemporary restoration has largely brought this building back to its 1840s appearance.

Cigar-making was an important industry in nineteenth-century New York, which employed thousands of people, including young men and women with few skills and little work experience. As Dorothy Richardson wrote in her book *The Long Day, the Story of a New York Working Girl* in 1905, "The advertisements for cigar and cigarette workers [in the city] were very numerous; and as that sounded like humble work, I thought I might stand a better chance in that line than any other." Although Richardson recounted having gone to a factory—filled with "a small army of boys and girls"—to apply for a job, cigars were also made in tenement apartments

and other homes. In the late nineteenth century, a failed attempt was made to limit home production of cigars, in an effort to improve work conditions as well as to protect consumers. Reform of cigar production was, however, unlikely at the very moment that the cigar had begun "its reign as the country's most popular tobacco product." By 1900 there were 6.7 billion cigars produced yearly in the United States under some 350,000 trade names,[1] among them the Starlight Bros. Company, the proprietors of the La Rosa de Paris Cigar Factory on Pearl Street in Lower Manhattan. Edward S. Innes was likely associated with a growing cigar-making business such as this.

Cigar factories were just some of the thousands of industrial establishments that existed in Manhattan in the nineteenth century. The increase in their numbers, as well as the expansions of other sectors of the economy following recovery from the financial Panic of 1837 exerted extreme pressure on the city's existing housing stock by the 1840s. After 1839, when townhouse construction in the city fell to less than half of what it had been before the Panic, house building increased steadily during the first half of the 1840s: In 1842, 912 rowhouses were constructed on speculation for sale to investors, while the next year some 1,273 went up, and by 1845 1,980 were built.[2] Innes was therefore participating in the housing boom of the 1840s, getting in just as the market was rebounding from its previous slump.

By the early 1840s, when Innes's row was constructed, the stylistic treatments of Greenwich Village townhouses had generally changed somewhat, although the typical plans were essentially unaltered from the Federal style. As published townhouse plans

Innes house facade.

had recommended in previous decades, the Greek Revival rowhouses of the 1840s generally had side entrances and stair halls with adjoining parlors on the main level. Since kitchens continued to be located on the lower level, as in this example, pantries were sometimes included at the center of the parlor level, between the front parlor, and the rear parlor, which was commonly used for dining. On the upper levels, the same spatial organization persisted with two main bedrooms at front and rear on each floor. The Greek Revival houses built in Manhattan as speculative rentals for artisans and others of similar means grafted stylish columns and other classicizing details onto an older conception of an urban house. Therefore, many of the Greek Revival houses were of a similar scale as the earlier dwellings and possessed the same brick facades and steeply pitched roofs punctuated by dormers. What had changed was the decorative treatment that was motivated by, in addition to other factors, American sympathy for the Greek cause in their War of Independence against the Ottoman Empire, which concluded in 1832.

Demand for housing did not abate as a result of the boom in residential construction in Manhattan (including Greenwich Village) during the 1840s. Throughout the nineteenth century, in spite of periodic economic crises, steady development of commercial activity created demand for housing that could not be met by new construction. This house, like many others, was divided into smaller apartments following the period of its original construction, and in response to functional changes and the critical disdain for certain aspects of the nineteenth-century rowhouse in later times, its stoop was removed by 1969 and a new entrance created at street level. By the mid-nineteenth century, the stoop had become such a ubiquitious and elaborate element of the New York rowhouse that in 1859

the city's ordinances had to limit the depth of the stoop to seven feet and its height to five feet. Despite how substantial they were, many stoops were later shorn off when they were deemed too "Victorian" in character. Not all New York townhouses have benefited from the kind of sympathetic restoration that the Innes house has witnessed.

The current owners purchased the house in 1980. Some sixteen years later, they embarked on a meticulous renovation project that lasted some five-and-a-half years, the aim of which was "to be as invisible as possible" (in the words of one of the owners) in the course of bringing the house back to a semblance of its original appearance. Because many original features had been lost when the house was converted to apartments, missing elements had to be based on those found in other buildings in the neighborhood. The owners worked tirelessly to locate appropriate local models wherever moldings or other decorative features had been lost and had to be replaced. The result is a house that to all appearances is original to its early 1840s date and Greek Revival style; however, it is in actuality a dedicated re-creation of the earlier form of the building, which had been largely lost as a consequence of changing uses through the nineteenth and twentieth centuries, a process of transformation that mirrors the larger fortunes of Greenwich Village as a residential neighborhood.

NOTES
1 Susan McCormick, "Banning Homework: A Case Study of Class, Community and State in the Fulton County Glove Industry," The Glovers of Fulton County Project, Department of History, University at Albany, c. 2002; Patricia A. Cooper, "What This Country Needs Is a Good Five-Cent Cigar," *Technology and Culture*, Vol. 29, no. 4 (Oct. 1988): 779–86.
2 Lockwood, *Bricks and Brownstone*, 76–77.

Front entrance and stairhall showing the wealth of period detail that has been restored.

The wallpaper is a reproduction of Zuber et Cie's New York Bay from their Vues d'Amerique du Nord (*1834*).

The dining room with restored marble fireplace surround and parquet floor.

Parlor with stone fireplace surround and mantelpiece.

Bookcases framed by columns exemplify the high level of detailing in the house.

Bedroom with marble fireplace surround.

Bathroom with delicate window details.

Samuel E. Bourne House

1842–43

This house is one of a pair constructed by "master builder" Andrew Lockwood. While the adjoining residence has been replaced by a later one, here the original Greek Revival building has been preserved. The history of its original construction speaks to the growth of New York City as a port following the opening of the Erie Canal in 1825, and of the resulting growth of Greenwich Village as a residential district.

Lockwood was a speculative builder who likely hoped to capitalize on the strong demand for housing in New York City in the 1840s that resulted from the growth of commercial activity after the canal was completed. The Erie Canal spawned the extension of other inland waterways on which goods were brought from the hinterlands to the city for consumption and export, while imports also traveled from New York to other destinations. International trade, including the China trade, brought new residents who profited from such commercial activity, while at the same time, the introduction of more reliable cross-seas passenger service contributed to a staggering increase in population during the antebellum period. For example, in 1830 the population of New York City was close to 200,000, and five years later it stood at more than 270,000. Such a rapid rise meant thousands of individuals and families needing housing, preferably close to the centers of economic activity.[1]

Samuel E. Bourne was a ship's captain who no doubt profited from the activity in New York's port in the 1830s and 1840s. His surname was a familiar one in northern New England, particularly on Cape Cod in Massachusetts and in coastal Maine, in the nineteenth century. He may well be the Samuel Bourne who was born in Weymouth, Massachusetts, in 1802, married Mary Bayley

Richards in 1825, and whose son Samuel Erastus Bourne was born in 1828. Presumably, he moved with his wife and young son to New York around the time that this house was built. If he relocated to New York to capitalize on the expanding shipping trade there, it would have been understandable given that the city's percentage of U.S. imports, just one indicator of maritime activity, grew by about half between 1821 and 1836, from 38 percent to 62 percent. In the port itself, the increase in trade was visible in the hundreds of ships docked there: "On a single day in 1836, 921 vessels lined the East River bulkhead, their bowsprits and carved figureheads looming over South Street, while another 320 bobbed along the Hudson (still known to sailors as the North River)." These vessels carried the goods that New York's 400-plus commercial firms imported and exported, and they also handled the goods that the city's 918 commission firms sent to other domestic destinations.[2] Vessels docked on the west side of Manhattan would have been readily accessible from Bourne's Greenwich Village residence.

Lockwood likely intended to attract a buyer from among the prosperous merchants and others who, like Bourne, profited from this expansion of trade in the first half of the nineteenth century. His decision to build a townhouse with the standard features of a side hall and double parlors on the main level, a kitchen and dining room on the lower floor, and bedrooms on the upper levels, demonstrates his awareness of what buyers' expectations were for an urban house of the period. Four stories in height and twenty feet wide, the Bourne house was not the largest in the neighborhood, but it did have some stylish Greek Revival details that would have attracted a fairly successful buyer. The

Bourne house facade.

Above: *View through the double parlors with neoclassical furnishings and a highly patterned carpet that are appropriate to the date and style of the house.*

Opposite: *Fireplace in the front parlor.*

eminent merchant and onetime mayor, Philip Hone, who played an important role in the development of Washington Square, was among the wealthy New Yorkers who were captivated by the Greek Revival, commenting in his journal on February 14, 1838, "How strange it is that in all the inventions of modern times architecture alone seems to admit of no improvement—every departure from the classical models of antiquity in this science is a departure from grace and beauty."

As appealing as the house and its location were for buyers in the 1840s, when Greenwich Village was later eclipsed by newer neighborhoods by mid-century, the house suffered substantial alterations. It was broken up into duplex apartments, and the loss of the neighboring house created structural problems that were only inadequately addressed. The present owners purchased the house in the mid-1980s and began a patient renovation of the interior. Because of its decrepit state, much of the interior was gutted and replaced. Wherever possible, intrinsic details were preserved. In those instances where the treatment had been lost, new features were patterned after surviving parts of the house, and by referring to the publications of Minard Lafever that seem to have guided the design of the building. Lafever was a New Jersey–born builder-architect who trained as a carpenter in New York State prior to setting up his own architectural practice in the city in 1828. The first modern historian of the Greek Revival movement, Talbot Hamlin, underscored the importance of Lafever's three first published books of designs—*The Young Builder's General Instructor* (1829), *The Modern Builder's Guide* (1833), and *The Beauties of Modern Architecture* (1835)—which, in a period when professional architects in the United States were scarce, provided images of Greek Revival details that were used by house builders anxious to fulfill their clients' demands for up-to-date designs. Hamlin summarized the impact the architect had on townhouse design, circumscribed as it in some senses was: "In New York houses the general plan and proportions were so fixed by the satisfactory traditional norm that the Greek inspiration could only be useful in details—how exquisitely may be seen in the beautiful and restrained plates of the Lafever books."[3] Pilastered window and door frames are among the Greek Revival details that distinguish this interior and that recall the period of the house's original construction, when New York's vibrant maritime economy provided opportunities for designers, builders, and urban residents.

NOTES
1 Edwin G. Burrows and Mike Wallace, *Gotham: A History of New York City to 1898* (New York: Oxford University Press, 1999), 430–35.
2 Ibid, 435.
3 Talbot Hamlin, *Greek Revival Architecture in America* (London: Oxford University Press, 1944), 146–48, 436; "A Classic Revision," *Historic Preservation*, Vol. 42, no. 2 (Mar. 1990): [46]–53.

The dining room is found at the front of the lower level, its traditional location in a nineteenth century Greenwich Village house.

Bedroom with decoration inspired by the nineteenth-century Aesthetic movement.

A stairhall with a niche at the upper level, used to display sculpture, was typical in the nineteenth century.

The modern kitchen is on at the lower level;
the dining table and chairs are designed by
George Nakashima.

View from the house toward the rear of the garden.

The back facade of the house with glass doors that open out from the kitchen.

Jeremiah Terbell House

1846–47

Dating to just a few years before Lady Emmeline Wortley's visit to the United States in 1849–50, this house represents the New York building boom of the 1840s, on which the British woman commented when she wrote that the city's streets were cluttered with "piles of lumber, mounds of brick, pyramids of stones, mountains of packing-cases, and stacks of goods." Lady Wortley conceded New York's beauty, nonetheless, when she wrote that it "certainly is handsome," but added this caveat: "yet there is something about it which gives the impression of a half-finished city."[1] At the time of Lady Wortley's trip, blocks of houses such as these were under construction or newly finished. To wealthy New Yorkers they represented speculative investment opportunities, and for the fairly well-off new-comers to the city (or the newly prosperous), they provided capacious and stylish accommodations in a fashionable neighborhood.

This property was owned by a series of investors during the first half of the nineteenth century when Greenwich Village witnessed intensive residential development. In 1825, the land itself was sold in a parcel of eighteen lots to a couple who had extensive property investments in Manhattan real estate: Mary Rhinelander and her husband, William C. Rhinelander. Although the Rhinelanders, prominent New Yorkers, sold this property to Jeremiah Terbell in 1846, they developed many other rental properties in Greenwich Village. In 1843 they built Rhinelander Row, a group of eleven houses with wooden porches across their facades that was a landmark on Seventh Avenue between Twelfth and Thirteenth streets until its demolition in 1937. After 1854, on West Eleventh Street, the couple built Rhinelander Gardens, an impressive group of eight rowhouses (now demolished). Attributed to architect James Renwick, the houses had connecting iron porches with Gothic Revival details at all three stories. The Rhinelanders would have been among the developers who added to the Manhattan building activity that Lady Wortley observed around 1850.

Jeremiah Terbell was not a speculator or investor, but instead lived in the house with his wife, Caroline Terbell, for two decades after completing it in 1847. The house, and an adjoining one built the next year, may have represented the work of Abraham Frazee, a mason. The Terbells demonstrated their awareness of current architectural fashion by building a house that, while consistent with other residences of the 1830s and 1840s in the Greek Revival style, nonetheless incorporated some features of the emerging Italianate idiom. Twenty-two feet wide (on the ample side of a moderately priced house of the period), the Terbell house has a traditional facade of brick, which had been employed in Federal and Greek Revival townhouses, and its ironwork at the stoop and areaway employs the familiar Greek Key motif. However, the basement level was faced with rusticated brownstone (scored to resemble more massive blocks of stone), as was that of the adjoining house where the treatment has been preserved, and the stoop and entrance enframement are likewise brownstone. The use of brownstone, and especially in its rusticated treatment, indicate the contemporary interest in Italian Renaissance architecture. The architects, builders, and owners of urban houses in New York and other cities were drawn, by the 1840s and 1850s, to the examples of the palaces of Renaissance Rome and Florence that had been characterized by warm-colored

Terbell house facade.

stone construction in which the constituent blocks were emphasized by rustication, giving them an almost fortresslike quality. The arched entrance doors with glass panels are also typical of the Italianate style and were likely installed in the 1850s or 1860s.

The interior of the house similarly reflects ideas about urban dwellings that were in transition in the 1840s. The plan is like those of earlier residences in Greenwich Village and elsewhere, but their uses may have been already evolving, for example with the rear parlor on the main floor being given over to dining, a function formerly relegated to the front basement rooms. Some decorative elements, such as the marble fireplace mantels on the parlor level, have Greek Revival characteristics, while others, such as some of the ceiling moldings, are typical of the Italianate style.

The house was sufficiently fashionable to attract other fairly prosperous owners after the Terbells' period of residence: Sheppard and Sarah Knapp, who purchased it in 1874. Knapp, operated Sheppard Knapp & Co., a carpet manufacturer and textile and furniture retailer located nearby. In 1875, *The New York Times* noted that Sheppard Knapp carried a wide array of upholstery and drapery fabric, as well as "fringes, gimps, cords and tassels for trimming lambrequins and draperies." These were essentials of a bourgeois Victorian interior, and as the company prospered, the Knapps and their extended family (which numbered eleven in 1880) moved uptown with other wealthy New Yorkers, finally ending up on Riverside Drive, on the Upper West Side.

When the Knapps left Greenwich Village for more fashionable quarters, they sold the house to Henrietta Starr, who with her husband, George, lived on West Thirteenth Street and rented this property to a clerk named William Frampton, whose wife, Emma, likely operated it as a rooming house. The Terbell house thus entered the cycle that many Greenwich Village houses experienced, wherein a formerly single-family house was converted to multiple units as the character of the neighborhood shifted.

Dining room with a scenic wallpaper in grisaille.

View through the double parlors toward the pier mirror at front.

The Framptons' boarders were largely working- or middle-class men, including several salesmen and a photographer in 1900.

The pattern of ownership of the Terbell house also followed neighborhood patterns with respect to the ethnicity of its owners. In 1903 it was purchased by Edward J. Donlin, an Irish-American doctor associated with Tammany Hall. Through his affiliation with the New York City Coroner's Office between 1889 and 1890, he gained prominence as a medical authority, testifying at a number of sensational murder trials that were widely publicized in their day. In the same year that he entered the Coroner's Office, Donlin married Annie E. McGinley and the couple eventually had five children. The five children lived in the house well into adulthood and the three unmarried sisters assumed ownership of it in 1930, three years before their father, a widower since before 1920, died. The large house, made even more spacious by a rear two-story addition from around 1880, could easily accommodate an extended family of adults. Thus the Donlins made few alterations to the house, although at the direction of the Donlin sisters, a formal plan for the rear garden was produced by R. Vaughn Watson, an engineer and landscape architect, who worked on the project with Humphrey Roger Avery's Swan River Nursery on Long Island.[2]

Despite many changes in ownership and use since it was first constructed, the Terbell house preserves much of its original character, especially due to the sensitive renovations of its current owners. The house testifies to the mid-nineteenth century boom in residential construction, as well as to the evolving character of Greenwich Village.

NOTES
1 Lady Emmeline Charlotte Elizabeth Stuart Wortley, *Travels in the United States . . . during 1849 and 1850* (London, 1851), 1, 2, quoted in Ellen W. Kramer, "Contemporary Descriptions of New York City and Its Public Architecture ca. 1850," *Journal of the Society of Architectural Historians*, Vol. 27, no. 4 (Dec. 1968): 269.
2 Eugene L. Armbruster, *Landmarks on the Montauk Highway* (Brooklyn, NY: [s.n.], 1925), 9; Andrew Scott Dolkart's unpublished research from 2003 on the Terbell House is the basis for much of the chronology of construction and ownership presented here.

Stairhall with a niche on the second-story landing.

The spaces at the center of the upper floors of large nineteenth-century rowhouses posed certain design challenges, such as the lack of direct sunlight. Here, the glazed windows in the doors closing off the bedrooms on either side help illuminate the dressing area between them, which is fitted with drawers and cupboards.

Bedroom with a marble fireplace and a nineteenth-century high-post bedstead.

Pocket doors connect upper level bedrooms, which are separated by a dressing room.

Built-in cabinets provide storage for the
kitchen and dining room.

Garden room with large windows allows plenty of sun exposure.

The rear facade of the house is covered with climbing roses.

Doorway into the rear garden.

Pen and Brush

(Abraham Bininger House), 1848

This house is significant as both a nineteenth-century residence, and as the home of the Pen and Brush, which began in 1892 as "the country's first organization of women artists and writers." The building's history illustrates the emergence, in the mid-nineteenth century, of Greenwich Village as a desirable residential neighborhood, as well as its preeminence by the end of the century as a center for artistic life in New York City.

In 1848 the house was built by a grocer and wine merchant named Abraham Bininger as his own expansive residence. The house was a grand one, in keeping with the Bininger family's remarkable success story. Abraham's grandfather (another Abraham Bininger) had immigrated from Switzerland to the United States, where he was orphaned shortly thereafter and educated at a Methodist school for orphans in Savannah, Georgia. Eventually, the elder Bininger became a Moravian minister, while his son Isaac fought in the Revolutionary War, was "finely educated," and eventually established a store in Camden Valley, New York, which was said to be "the most extensive between Albany and Montreal." Isaac's son, Abraham M. Bininger (1800–1870), the builder of this house, was associated with the successful A. M. Bininger & Co., a wine and liquor retail establishment. Bininger showed his business acumen by buying wine and spirits from their producers, then retailing them in distinctive colored bottles that bore the company name. (The bottles are avidly collected today.) At the time of his death, it was reported that Abraham Bininger claimed to be "the original Hapsburg Bininger, as he no doubt is, for he was the hereditary owner of Bininger Castle, its portraits, old furniture, and rare old wills and title-deeds, at Salem, N.Y." Abraham was one of the family members who had amassed a substantial fortune through the "great Bininger grocery-houses." At his death he left an estate valued at $250,000 or more.[1]

This grand house was built when Bininger was in his late forties, at the height of his economic fortunes. High ceilings, opulent details, and expensive materials (for example, the marble used for the mantelpieces on the parlor floor) bespeaks the wealth of the original owner. It is also stylistically quite up-to-date, illustrating the transition from the earlier Greek Revival style—which predominated for rowhouse design in the 1830s and 1840s—to the Italianate style that accompanied the emergence of brownstone as a preferred material for the facades of city houses in the 1850s.

NOTES
1 "Strange, Eventful History," *The New York Times* (Oct. 15, 1870): 2.

Window with Gothic-style tracery at the rear of the parlor.

View through the double parlors.

*Former parlor (now the gallery) with the
original marble mantelpiece.*

These original double doors with arched panels and moldings are characteristic of the Italianate style.

Front entrance and stairhall. The bulbous turnings on the balusters of the stair's handrail represent a departure from the tapered elements found on the stairs of earlier houses.

Right: Gothic-style library at the rear of the parlor level.

Opposite: The library has traceried paneling and ceiling details that recall Gothic rib vaulting.

James Phalen House

1850–51

Greenwich Village since its beginnings has provided real-estate investment opportunities, regardless of how the neighborhood has changed. This house reflects mid-nineteenth century real-estate investment in the Village, but its history also provides a window onto the broader evolution of the neighborhood from a middle-class residential district to a Bohemian enclave by the early twentieth century.

The house was originally built for the estate of James Phalen, likely as an income-producing rental property. Like other nearby brick houses, this one is four stories high and modestly ornamented at the facade. In keeping with its mid-century date, it has a rusticated basement. Its side-hall plan, and two principal rooms on each floor, reflect well-established townhouse formulae.

Like many other Greenwich Village houses, this one originally had a passage to the rear of the property, which provided access to Pamela Court where a back house had been built for Albert Romaine in 1827. Later, after an adjoining house was remodeled in 1927 to provide a proper entrance from the street, Pamela Court became renowned as the location of a legendary Prohibition-era "speakeasy." It was more or less an open secret at such Village establishments that liquor was served in teacups. Outlawing alcoholic beverages did not prevent New Yorkers from becoming publicly "stinko," "sqiffy," "owled," or any number of other synonyms that Edmund Wilson listed for intoxicated in his "Lexicon of Prohibition" (1927).[1]

Several years after Wilson drew up his list of terms for drunkenness, the French diplomat and writer Paul Morand provided a description of a period speakeasy in his book New York: "The speakeasy . . . is a clandestine refreshment-bar selling spirits or wine. The door is closed, and is only opened after you have been scrutinized through a door-catch or barred opening." Morand continued, "There is a truly New York atmosphere or humbug in the whole thing. The interior [of the speakeasy] is that of a criminal house; shutters are closed in full daylight, and one is caught in the smell of a cremation furnace."[2] Among the habitués of the speakeasy at Pamela Court were the literary figures Theodore Dreiser, John Dos Passos, and Edna St. Vincent Millay. Millay, who was originally from Rockland, Maine, moved to Greenwich Village after graduating from Vassar College and became one of the neighborhood's most celebrated figures. Her architectural claim to fame is for having lived in 1923–24 at 75 1/2 Bedford Street, a building that is often referred to as "the narrowest house in New York City." Built in 1873 to fill a carriage entrance to a stable located on a back lot, it is only nine-and-a-half feet wide. There, Millay collaborated with Deems Taylor on the opera The King's Henchman, which was performed at the Metropolitan Opera.[3]

This more ample house has been carefully renovated as a single-family residence. Despite the addition of a modern kitchen and bathrooms, it retains much of its original detailing and certainly preserves the atmosphere of a mid-century Greenwich Village residence of moderate scale.

NOTES
1 Ann Douglas, Terrible Honesty (New York: Farrar, Straus, and Giroux, 1995), 101.
2 Paul Morand, New York, 1925, Hamish Miles, trans. (New York: H. Holt and Co., 1930); quoted in Michael and Ariane Batterberry, On the Town in New York (New York and London: Routledge, 1999), 203.
3 Miller, Greenwich Village, 202.

Phalen house facade.

Original fireplace details contrast with modernist furnishings in a sitting area.

A corner of the front parlor with a glimpse of the street beyond. The furnishings range from the eighteenth-century French chair to a modern sofa.

*The sitting and dining areas adjacent to the kitchen
overlook the rear yard.*

*A marble-topped peninsula in the kitchen blends
with the house's historic character.*

Stairhall showing a replacement handrail of metal that blends with the house's original, rather austere aesthetic.

View into the stairhall from a bedroom.

Salmagundi Club

(Irad Hawley House), 1852–53

Home today of the Salmagundi Club, this house is among the grand residences built on lower Fifth Avenue at the middle of the nineteenth century. It is the unique survivor of a collection of mid-century houses that once constituted the Manhattan stronghold of New York society as chronicled in the novels of Edith Wharton.

Following the development of large-scale, high-style Greek Revival houses on the north side of Washington Square, Henry Brevoort, Jr. built a mansion at the northwest corner of Fifth Avenue and Ninth Street in 1834 that established the area's social prominence. Later, Brevoort built a row of eight houses nearby on West Eleventh Street, while a New Orleans merchant named Hart M. Shiff built a mansion, close by on Fifth Avenue, in 1852. Designed by architect Detlef Lienau, the house featured a mansard roof and echoed the then-current French Second Empire style. James Renwick, a prominent architect of churches and other institutions in New York and elsewhere, is thought to have designed the house his parents occupied in 1851 at the southeast corner of Ninth Street. These were among the large residences that lent the area just north of Washington Square its architectural and social cache, not to mention its architectural character, which was secured by a number of fine churches, including the 1840–41 Church of the Ascension by Richard Upjohn at the northwest corner of Fifth Avenue and Tenth Street. The Gothic Revival First Presbyterian by architect Joseph C. Wells was completed on the west side of Fifth Avenue between Eleventh and Twelfth Streets in 1846. Just north of the church, on the opposite side of Fifth Avenue, James Lenox, an elder and benefactor of the church, built an enormous Gothic Revival house.[1]

While the Lenox house had a frontage of seventy-two feet on Fifth Avenue, by way of contrast, the house that Irad Hawley, the president of the Pennsylvania Coal Company, built on the east side of Fifth Avenue, between Eleventh and Twelfth Streets, stretched some thirty-nine feet across the avenue and its lot extended back 125 feet. As expansive as the Hawley house appears in comparison to the relatively modest nineteenth-century rowhouses in Greenwich Village, others were even larger. The Hawley house, however, embodied on an expanded scale many features of the New York Italianate townhouse. On the most fundamental level, it reflects the growing taste for brownstone as a building material at the middle of the nineteenth century, a phenomenon that Edith Wharton lamented when she wrote in her novel *The Age of Innocence* of "the brownstone of which the uniform hue coated New York like a cold chocolate sauce." The ubiquity of the material led some to speak of a veritable "Brownstone Blitz" that struck the city in the 1850s and 1860s. Like smaller brownstones, the Hawley house has wide moldings around the windows, heavy lintels above the windows, an arched door opening, and a triangular pediment above the door, supported by large brackets.

On the interior, the house likewise mirrored smaller residences in its plan, but on an expanded scale. As in smaller residences, in the Hawley house there are double parlors on the main floor, joined by an arched opening framed by columns. The size of the house allows for pairs of pilasters and columns on each side of an arched opening. The elabo-

View through the grandly scaled and delicately detailed stairhall. The extraordinary level of finish is indicated by the molded "panels" below each flight of stairs.

rateness of this treatment is complemented by heavy plaster detailing at the ceiling. The front parlor possesses a marble mantelpiece supported by three-dimensional figures, of a type that became popular among wealthy homeowners by the 1850s.[2] Like other large houses in Greenwich Village built from the mid-century onward, the Hawley house had a dining room overlooking the yard at the rear. The dining room has been reused as gallery space for the Salmagundi Club.

The Salmagundi Club fulfilled a particular need in the New York art world of the late nineteenth century as a venue that focused not on grand-scale paintings, but rather on smaller sketches and works in other media. As *The New York Times* commented on the occasion of the institution's 1880 show: "This second formal exhibition of the Salmagundi Club establishes the society in the good graces of the public. It supplies a want felt even more by artists than the public, and encourages workmen, if not in the highest spheres of high art, yet in a more modest sphere, where all the genius a man possesses can come in play and not be [too] great for the vehicle of his thought." Over the years, the club was felt to have lost its bohemian character, as is suggested by illustrations in an article published in *Scribner's Monthly* in 1880. Two sketches, titled "The Salmagundi Club in Early Times" by Will H. Low, and "A Modern Meeting of the Salmagundi Club" by H. P. Share, contrasted a raucous garret meeting of bearded *artistes* with a sober evening of well-dressed gentlemen. In both cases, however, the walls were plastered with smallish works of art, presumably produced by the members. In 1880, the Salmagundi club was meeting Friday nights "at the studio of a young marine

painter in Astor Place. The appurtenances are somewhat dingy, and there is a mellow atmosphere of smoke in the room." The club was still quite informal and opposed to official hierarchies: "Red-tapeism is made odious." The topics for the sketches produced by the members on such occasions were selected by vote from among proposed themes such as "Yes or No," "Idolatry," "Silence," or "Blood," among others. The resulting works were then critiqued at the Art Students League, "for a formal exposition by a professor of the principles of design exhibited in them. With all this the once happy-go-lucky Salmagundi Club may well flatter itself on having become one of the most improving agencies in the whole artistic community."[3]

The Salmagundi Club remained in its West Twelfth Street home for about twenty years, until 1917 when it purchased its current building from the estate of William G. Park for around $100,000. Enthusiasm for the project was high among the members who, as *The New York Times* reported on several occasions that February, produced paintings that were auctioned to help fund the purchase. Not only did they support the club's activities, they also ensured the preservation of one of the Village's great mansions.

NOTES
1 Luther S. Harris, *Around Washington Square*, 109–117; Lockwood, *Bricks and Brownstone*, 189–91.
2 Amelia Peck, "The Products of Empire: Shopping for Home Decoration in New York City," Voorsanger and Howat, eds., *Art and the Empire City*, 260–65.
3 "The Salmagundi Club," *The New York Times* (Jan. 20, 1880): 5; William H. Bishop, "Young Artists' Life in New York," *Scribner's Monthly*, Vol. 19, issue 3 (Jan. 1880): 355–69.

Stairhall decorated with the work of club members and portraits of officials.

The club's library, looking toward the street, with its preserved memorabilia.

Fireplace in the club's library with an elaborate marble mantelpiece. Some of the former members' palettes hang above the bookcase to the right.

Above: An intricately carved marble mantelpiece, which would have been found in only the largest nineteenth-century Greenwich Village houses.

Opposite: Archway between the first-floor parlors, supported by Corinthian columns.

Walter W. Price House

1866

This house stands on land that once comprised a portion of the estate of the wealthy merchant Abraham Van Nest, who purchased it in 1821. Originally, Van Nest's property was part of the country seat, called "Greenwich House," of Admiral Sir Peter Warren whose property was divided after his death in 1752 and later developed. Warren had married Susannah DeLancey, of a prominent New York family, in 1731 and later led the British squadron at the 1745 siege of Louisbourg. In the wake of that battle, when cash was short in New England, Warren made a number of loans there and elsewhere that contributed to his wealth.[1] The establishment of Warren's estate, and the continued use of a portion of it as a country seat by Van Nest, meant that a significant amount of property in Greenwich Village would be available for development in the second half of the nineteenth century. The houses built on this property reflected the tastes and economics of the period.

Walter W. Price built not just this house, but the two flanking houses as well, in the wake of the Civil War. Although the building project was undoubtedly a speculative undertaking, Price and his family lived in this house, although only for a few years before selling it (at a profit) to his partner in a brewery, Ernest G. W. Woerz. The latter was described by *The New York Times* at the time of his son's marriage in 1888, as a "wealthy brewer," who was able to collaborate with the bride's parents in giving the newlyweds a large brick-and-brownstone house on East Eightieth Street on the fashionable Upper East Side as a wedding present. Real estate investment had likely helped Price and Woerz become even more prosperous than they already were as a consequence of New York's thriving brewery

industry. In the second half of the nineteenth century, huge amounts of hops were grown in New York State, much of it going to beer making in the state and particularly in New York City where there were numerous breweries, many run by German immigrants.[2] The Price house was later owned by members of another family with connections to the liquor business, that of John H. Gerdes, a German immigrant who had liquor concessions in taverns and whose family owned the house from the 1880s through the 1960s.

Large and imposing, the Price house represented the transformation of the rowhouse plan that took place in New York City in the 1860s. The expansive width of the house allows for some deviation from the previously familiar rowhouse plan in which a side stair hall typically provided access to double parlors at the main level. Here, as in other large houses of similar date, the double doors at the entrance lead to a vestibule with a stair hall beyond, flanked at one side by a parlor and leading at the rear to a dining room that runs the width of the house across the back. The dining room overlooking the backyard took the place of the so-called tearoom that was a feature of earlier rowhouses; often that room had been framed in wood and conceived of separately from the masonry block of the house.[3] Replacing the tearoom with the rear dining room offered the advantage of avoiding creating a dark space at the center of the plan. It also put the dining room at the end of the axis formed by the stair hall. In this house, the parlor and dining room display the most elaborate decorative treatment in the entire building—their painted ceilings—which are rare survivals from the nineteenth century, having been restored in recent decades. Unusual today,

Iron railing and gate at the lower-level street entrance.

Price house facade. Its high stoop and heavily bracketed door hood are characteristic of New York rowhouses of the period.

such decoration was apparently ubiquitous in the period, since in 1854 *Putnam's Monthly* could declare that "Painted ceilings, gilded cornices, and floors of colored marbles, or inlaid with vari-colored woods were once very rare, even in the houses of the wealthiest merchants; but now these elegancies are so common that their absence would be much more likely to excite remark than their presence."[4]

Stylistically, the Price house represents tastes in rowhouse design that were current in the 1860s. It combines two popular materials: brick (which had been used for rowhouses in previous decades) and stone for the English basement. The architect was working at a moment when brownstone was a popular facing material for townhouses throughout New York, thoroughly transforming the appearance of newly developed neighborhoods on both the east and west sides of Upper Manhattan. The architect also demonstrated his familiarity with the popular Second Empire style by employing a mansard roof as well as segmental arches over the windows and doorway.

Gage E. Inslee (d. 1895), the architect of this house, practiced in New York and designed a number of impressive brownstones on the Upper East Side in the decade following this commission. (Evidently, he was pursuing wealthy clients uptown as those neighborhoods outstripped Greenwich Village in desirability.) However, Inslee was also responsible for some significant public buildings in the metropolitan area, including the Congregational Church in Stamford, Connecticut, from around 1858 and the First Baptist Church in the same city from 1859–60. While the Price house is Second Empire in style, Inslee was conversant with a variety of historical idioms, ranging from medieval Romanesque to Italian Renaissance classicism. Indeed, the Baptist church in Stamford has been considered an example of "creative fantasy" in the combination of historical forms in that Inslee brought together in the one building an array of arches and ceiling vaults inspired by different moments in the history of Western architecture.[5]

Recent renovations have adapted the house to modern requirements. For instance, the subbasement was excavated to provide space for an exercise room and laundry facilities, while at the basement level, the kitchen was modernized and opened onto the rear yard. The deep property backs up to others that are likewise quite extensive, thus creating ample space for a treed garden. Mostly invisible from the streets, such gardens have long been treasured in Greenwich Village, for example, by Anna Alice Chapin, who recounted many paeans to such places in her book *Greenwich Village* (1917). Chapin herself considered the gardens of Greenwich Village as metaphors for the community itself, writing, "[T]hey do blossom, those hidden and usually unfruitful garden-places. Sometimes they bloom in real flowers that anyone can see and touch and smell. Sometimes they come only as flowers of the heart—which, after all, will do as well as another sort,—in Greenwich Village, where they know how to make believe."

NOTES
1 Julian Gwyn, "Money Lending in New England: The Case of Admiral Sir Peter Warren and His Heirs, 1739–1805," *The New England Quarterly*, Vol. 44, no. 1 (Mar. 1971): 117–34.
2 G. William Beardslee, "When Hops Were King," *New York State Archives* (Fall 2006): 18; When the firm of Beadleston & Woerz was incorporated in 1889 it was capitalized at nearly a million dollars (*The New York Times* [Jan. 6, 1889]).
3 Lockwood, *Bricks and Brownstone*, 167–68.
4 "New-York Daguerreotyped," *Putnam's Monthly*, Vol. III, no. XV (March 1854): 245.
5 Carroll V. Meeks, "Romanesque before Richardson in the United States," *The Art Bulletin* Vol. 35, no. 1 (Mar. 1953): 30–31.

Opposite: Parlor with elaborate paint and gilding and a marble mantelpiece.

Overleaf: Kitchen at the lower level with windows onto the garden.

Lower-level office.

*Dining room at the rear of the parlor level,
(now used to play pool) overlooking the garden.*

Cherner-O'Neill House
1801 (renovated 2003)

This glass-enclosed rooftop aerie pushes the boundaries of the Village at the same time that it challenges conventional ideas of what an urban residence can be. Located in the so-called Alphabet City (where the avenues are named "A," "B," "C," and so on) in the East Village, beyond the extent of Greenwich Village proper, the house is also the furthest thing from the modest brick-built rows of the early nineteenth century; it brings modernism to the domestic architecture of the Villages.

In a classic Manhattan evolution, as Greenwich Village became increasingly unaffordable to the very people who might have wanted to live there—artists and intellectuals—creative individuals lured by the Village's bohemian reputation moved beyond the neighborhood's former eastern boundary at Third Avenue, from where the El was removed in 1955. In 1952 writer Allen Ginsberg moved to 206 East Seventh Street, where his apartment became a meeting place for the Beat Generation. Since Ginsberg was the member of the group who had steady employment, and hence an apartment, other Beats regularly lived with him, including Gregory Corso, the first to move in, who was displaced in 1953 by Jack Kerouac. Other writers in the East Village in the 1950s included the poet W. H. Auden, and Norman Mailer. As others followed, the area was promoted by real estate brokers, who by 1961 were calling what had formerly been considered the Lower East Side, the "East Village." From the 1960s through the 1980s, the East Village became the site of a vibrant alternative arts scene that embraced music as well as the visual arts, including graffiti art in the 1980s and was the home of a vital gay community.[1] Today, the East Village is liberally defined by some to extend as far east as FDR Drive, and to include the largely Hispanic area between Avenues A and D, which is also referred to as "Loisaida" (echoing the Puerto Rican pronunciation of Lower East Side: "low-ees-side-ah").

Some greeted the transformation of the East Village enthusiastically, while others have decried the area's gentrification, which has made it less affordable to an ethnically, racially, and economically diverse population. As sociologist Sharon Zukin cautioned in *The New York Times* in 1977, with respect to the conversion to residential use of large swaths of formerly industrial properties in Lower Manhattan, "a much more critical appraisal must be made of the dynamics of the urban real estate market, particularly as affected by a wholesale process of renewal, reconstruction, and recodification of the use of space." Terry Miller was somewhat more sanguine about the gentrification of the East Village when he wrote in 1990 that "Bohemia is a hardy flower. Once it takes root in an area, it is persistent and all but impossible to eradicate"[2]—more like a weed, actually.

When Ben Cherner and Emma O'Neill, both of whom are architects in practice in New York City, purchased an early nineteenth century townhouse in the East Village with a group of friends, Alphabet City, as Cherner has said, was "a gentrifying area." The five couples planned to turn the building into four apartments, in part by extending the structure twenty feet into the rear of the property, and Cherner and O'Neill imagined constructing a penthouse that would entirely cover the roof. Structural issues, however, precluded such a large penthouse, and meant that a part of the roof could only be used as a deck. This limitation to an addition of twenty-by-twenty-five feet plus an entry provided an impetus for Cherner's and O'Neill's design, in which the boundaries between indoor and outdoor spaces are hardly distinguishable, and in which the available living area is treated with an eye toward efficiency that recalls a boat's interior.

Two-story living area with loft.

Nonetheless, O'Neill has said that she and Cherner resisted treating the house as a ship's cabin, choosing not to build in furnishings but instead to use freestanding tables and bureaus: "It was very important that it didn't feel like we were making the most out of the space."[3]

A perception of spaciousness results from the soaring dimensions of the main living space. The permissible height made it possible to insert a mezzanine into the penthouse that added a third more square footage on top of what was provided by the main floor of just under one thousand square feet. The mezzanine, accessed by a steel ladder that recalls the neighborhood's partly industrial character, provided a location for a bedroom and bathroom that overlook the living room, but gain privacy through a screen of black walnut into which are deftly cut hinged sections that can open and close.

The defining characteristics of the space are its lightness and the sensation it produces in the inhabitant or visitor of being perched atop the building, overlooking the adjacent park. (The urban gardens and small-scale parks of Loisaida are highly valued by the community and have been defended against development, with varying degrees of success.) Filling the interior with sun are the large bronze-framed windows scavenged from the Gucci Building on Fifth Avenue, renovated by Studio Sofield, where O'Neill was design director when the penthouse was constructed. The pivoting windows extend nearly to the floor and provide access to the deck on the street (north) side of the penthouse and expansive openings to the southern and western exposures that bathe the interior in sun, especially in the fall and winter when the trees in the adjoining park lose their leaves.

The modernist architecture is complemented by the furnishings, which include the molded-plywood "Cherner Chair" designed by Ben's father, Norman Cherner, for the Plycraft Company in 1958. Norman Cherner was educated at Columbia University and went on to teach there and to become an

View into the main living area.

instructor at the Museum of Modern Art between 1947 and 1949. As an architect, Cherner was an innovator in prefabricated housing but became well known for his furniture designs as well. Bowing to demand from fellow architects, in 1999 Ben Cherner formed the Cherner Chair Company with his brother Thomas, with the intention of reissuing some of their father's designs, including his much-admired chair. Although the modernist design of the penthouse marks a departure from much of the residential architecture of the East Village, the structure and its furnishings continue a long tradition of aesthetic innovation in Greenwich Village.

NOTES
1 Barry Miles, "The Beat Generation in the Village," *Greenwich Village: Culture and Counterculture*, Beard and Berlowitz, eds.
2 Sharon Zukin, "In Defense of Benign Neglect and Diversity," *The New York Times* (Feb. 13, 1977): 4; Miller, *Greenwich Village and How It Got That Way*, 279.
3 Marc Kristal, "Real Estate Magic in Alphabet City," *Dwell* (June 2002): 18, 20; Katy Dunn, "Mid-Century Magic," *Grand Design* (June 2006).

Opposite: Kitchen with the mezzanine above. Panels in the wall can be closed for privacy.

Below: Looking into the living area from the kitchen.

Above and opposite: Views into the living area.

Opposite: Metal stairs access the mezzanine-level bedroom.

Below: Bedroom with adjustable wood panels that open onto the main living space.

Modernist House

2005

Among the newest houses in Greenwich Village is this modernist work designed by architect Matthew Baird. It is a testament to the continuing architectural vitality of Greenwich Village, as well as to its desirability as a family neighborhood. The house's slivers of windows on the street facade and its expanses of glass at the rear provide views across the varied cityscape of northern Greenwich Village and a prospect over the full spectrum of architectural types and styles in the neighborhood.

The house's modernist aesthetic and industrial materials are appropriate to its location at the edge of the newly gentrified Meatpacking District. The market stands on the site of the former Fort Gansevoort, which was built in 1811 and named for the Revolutionary hero General Peter Gansevoort. After the fort was demolished in 1849, the site was used as a railroad yard and appropriated by farmers as an ersatz city market. Market buildings were constructed in the 1880s but the Gansevoort Market was demolished in 1950, replaced soon after by the Gansevoort Meat Center,[1] which has continued to lend the neighborhood its distinctive character despite the incursions of sophisticated shops, gourmet restaurants, and boutique hotels into the area.

Baird's clients discovered the site soon after moving to New York City with their family in 2001. On it was an extremely dilapidated Federal-period house,[2] of which traces remain in the form of portions of its masonry foundations in the new building. The house preserves the dimensions of the former house, which was built out to the full depth of the property, but the new structure substitutes open soaring spaces for the boxy rooms of early nineteenth-century rowhouses, and concrete and steel for the familiar

brick of other Greenwich Village houses.

The spatial excitement of the house begins at the basement level with a multi-height media room. At the street level is located a small office, mudroom, and garage (the latter a concession to Greenwich Village congestion). Above that is the most public level of the house with a living area facing toward the street, a kitchen in the middle of the space, and a dining area at the rear. The back wall of the dining area is almost completely glass and is designed so that it can open and fold back against itself, creating nearly total openness to the deck that is located above the media room on the lower level. The upper two floors are comprised of children's bedrooms and a master suite on the top floor. A variety of window openings and skylights fill the space with natural light and emphasize the striking geometry of the architecture.

Among the most striking aspects of the design is the facade, which is largely composed of a plate of steel forty feet high and fourteen feet wide affixed to it. Its seventeen-ton weight is belied by the effect that comes from its having been attached to the facade at a plane slightly beyond that of the windows at either side.[3] The sheet of steel is appropriate to a neighborhood that is characterized by a mixture of small-scale residential structures as well as larger industrial and commercial buildings. The material echoes the loft buildings one sees from the windows of the house as well as the nearby markets with their sheet-metal awnings and doors.

The sheet-metal plate registers on the interior only as an expanse of light-colored wall. It provides privacy from the street while the narrow windows at the corners of the facade offer glimpses up and down the neighborhood. The effect on the interior of seeming

Modernist house facade. The metal plate on the façade provides a transition between the loft buildings to the left and the early, small-scale townhouses to the right.

Stone and concrete mingle in the wall, showing how the modernist house builds on the earlier structure.

Main living space.

to hang over the street is likened by one of the owners to the spatial effects of another well-known design by Baird, the American Museum of Folk Art, for which he was project architect for the firm of Tod Williams and Billie Tsien. The museum, located on West Fifty-third Street in Midtown Manhattan, opened to great acclaim in late 2001. The facade of the Folk Art Museum is composed of sixty-three panels made of tombasil (a white bronze alloy). The architects arrived at this slightly textured material after having experimented with a variety of options. The tombasil was cast directly on the concrete floor of the foundry, which gave it a kind of hand-crafted feeling appropriate to the museum.

The facade of this house is smoother, but equally appropriate to the building's setting and function. While it echoes the commercial and industrial architecture that surrounds it, the house preserves the scale of Greenwich Village's nineteenth-century domestic architecture. It shows how the neighborhood still attracts artistic innovators and their patrons and demonstrates how cutting-edge buildings can be successfully integrated into a historic district without compromising the architectural integrity of the existing urban fabric.

NOTES
1 Miller, *Greenwich Village*, 154–55.
2 Lauren MacIntyre, "Housing Dept., Build Your Own," The Talk of the Town, *The New Yorker* (Jan. 12, 2004).
3 "Matthew Baird, Greenwich Street House, New York, New York, U.S.A.," *GA Houses* 86 (Mar. 2005): 180–83; Roger Yee, "Raising the Iron Curtain," *Oculus* Vol. 65, no. 4 (winter 2003–2004): 42.

Opposite: The soaring media room at the lower level.

Left: The dining area with deck beyond.

Concrete stair leading up to the second floor
from the kitchen.

View from the kitchen into the living area.

Above: A nineteenth-century Italian mosaic was incorporated
into the wall below the stair and now looks like a fragment
preserved from an earlier building on this site.

Opposite: The dining area and deck.

Lambert Suydam Row

1839

Behind the uniform rows of Greenwich Village houses are frequently found green oases recalling the neighborhood's earliest history. In his 1910 futuristic book, *The Mayor of New York*, Louis Pope Gratacap predicted how desirable the then-dilapidated houses of the Village would eventually become, in part by virtue of their gardens. He imagined how, in the years 1999 and 2000, the mayor would have "his official home in a beautifully reconstructed house in the Ninth Ward, how he was imitated by others until a flourishing and lovely neighborhood sprang up with gardens, trees, and a semi-rural charm recalling the ancient days." While the mayor's residence never migrated to Greenwich Village, the neighborhood did indeed attract new residents at the turn of the twenty-first century who were often lured by the gardens that were still preserved behind the streets of rowhouses.

Both this house and the one following (see page 211), with their gardens, formed parts of nineteenth-century rows that reflected a prevalent taste for architectural uniformity that predominated at the time. Lambert Suydam, a former president of the Manhattan Gas Light Company, later president of the New York Equitable Fire Insurance Company, and a trustee of the Greenwich Savings Bank between 1842 and 1848,[1] built his row of eight Greek Revival houses in 1839. Originally, the houses were three-and-a-half stories in height, although in most cases they have been raised

to a full four stories. The addition of another full story made what were already large houses even more grand. Their desirability was undoubtedly originally enhanced by their fine detailing, especially around the doorways.

This house in Suydam's row and its neighbor were later connected and substantially altered in 1957 when they became a convent. Around the year 2000, in response to the great desirability of Greenwich Village as a residential neighborhood (predicted ninety years earlier by Gratacap), the two houses were again separated and renovated as single-family homes. In the course of its rehabilitation, this house had its kitchen moved from the lower level, where it would traditionally have been found, to the rear of the parlor level. From there it enjoys a spectacular view over the rear garden. A low stone wall creates two levels in the garden, thereby making it appear more expansive than it truly is. Varieties of flowering plants provide a changing display throughout the growing season.

The renovation of the house transformed it into a large and comfortable family home. Its garden provides play areas for children, including a brightly-colored playhouse.

NOTES
1 *History of the Greenwich Savings Bank, New York* (New York: np, 1896), 36.

Facade of the Suydam Row house. Its garden is featured on the following pages.

View from the kitchen at the rear of the first story toward the front of the house.

A sitting area overlooking the balcony and garden.

Below: A balcony off of the kitchen provides a view of the garden.

Opposite: Low walls create a variety of planting and sitting areas in the garden.

Sitting area in the garden.

A colorful children's playhouse in the garden.

Linus Scudder Row

1851–52

A row of seven brick houses was built in 1851–52 by Linus Scudder, a mason and builder. Scudder appears to have been relatively successful since he was taxed on real estate valued at $41,200 in 1857.[1] By that date Scudder, who played an important role in the development of Greenwich Village from the time that he began working as a mason in 1836, had sold the four lots in the row that he had purchased from Timothy Whittemore, the president of the Greenwich Insurance Company. Scudder built houses for the families to whom he sold his lots, as well as those for adjoining homeowners in the row. By using the same builder, the homeowners ensured that their residences would all look the same, thereby giving the row a degree of grandeur. Like many houses in Greenwich Village, this one in the Scudder row was later divided into apartments and the entrance relocated to the ground level.

The full floor apartment at the lower level of one of the Scudder rowhouses enjoys access to the garden at the rear. The garden behind this house maintains the reputation of being one of the finest in Greenwich Village. Although the garden has evolved over many years, and has had several different designs, it is now focused primarily on roses. Focal points in the garden are created by structures modeled on those in a garden in Wales. Over them cascade a wide variety of roses whose vivid colors provide a strong visual counterpoint to the bright colors of the apartment interior.

Although the interior space is relatively small, the owner, a designer, changes the textiles and other details with the seasons. She thus mirrors the changing display in the garden, which effectively doubles the apartment's space during the spring and summer months.

Opposite: Work and storage areas in this small apartment are disguised by dramatic decorative objects and paneled doors.

Above: A focal point in the garden with hostas in the foreground.

NOTES

1 *Boyd's New York City Tax-book* ([New York]: W.H. Boyd, 1857), 177.

A collection of modern art and antique furnishings enlivens the small spaces in this apartment.

The dining area doubles as a library with built-in book-shelves. Nineteenth-century transfer-printed ceramics are used decoratively.

In the garden, roses contrast with colorful leafy foliage, such as coleus and sweet-potato vine.

A seating area in the garden.

Rose garden in full bloom.

Looking from the garden toward the back of the house.

Selected Bibliography

Banes, Sally, *Greenwich Village 1963: Avant-Garde Performance and the Effervescent Body.* Durham, NC: Duke University Press, 1993.

Barnes, Djuna. *Greenwich Village as It Is.* 1916. New York: Phoenix Bookshop, 1978.

Barnet, Andrea. *All Night Party: The Women of Bohemian Greenwich Village and Harlem, 1913–1930.* Chapel Hill, NC: Algonquin Books of Chapel Hill, 2004.

Beard, Rick and Leslie Cohen Berlowitz, eds. *Greenwich Village: Culture and Counterculture.* New Brunswick, NJ: Rutgers University Press for the Museum of the City of New York, 1993.

Blackmar, Elizabeth. *Manhattan for Rent, 1785–1850.* Ithaca and London: Cornell University Press, 1989.

Burrows, Edwin G. and Mike Wallace. *Gotham: A History of New York City to 1898.* New York: Oxford University Press, 1999.

Cantor, Mindy, ed. *Around the Square, 1830–1890.* New York: New York University Press, 1982.

Caro, Robert. *The Power Broker: Robert Moses and the Fall of New York.* New York: Knopf, 1974.

Carter, David. *Stonewall: The Riots that Sparked the Gay Revolution.* New York: St. Martin's, 2005.

Delaney, Edmund T. *New York's Greenwich Village.* Barre, MA: Barre Publishers, 1968.

Dell, Floyd. *Love in Greenwich Village.* New York: Doran, 1926.

Erenberg, Lewis A. *Steppin' Out: New York Nightlife and the Transformation of American Culture, 1890–1930.* Chicago: University of Chicago Press, 1984.

Gray, Christopher and Suzanne Braley. *New York Streetscapes: Tales of Manhattan's Significant Buildings and Landmarks.* New York: Harry N. Abrams, 2003.

Harris, Luther S. *Around Washington Square: An Illustrated History of Greenwich Village.* Baltimore and London: The Johns Hopkins University Press, 2003.

Jacobs, Jane. *The Death and Life of Great American Cities.* New York: Random House, 1961.

James, Henry. *Around Washington Square.* New York: Harper Bros., 1881.

Lockwood, Charles. *Bricks and Brownstone.* 1972. 2nd ed. New York: Rizzoli, 2003.

McFarland, Gerald W. *Inside Greenwich Village: A New York City Neighborhood, 1898–1918.* Amherst, MA: University of Massachusetts Press, c. 2001.

McKenna, H. Dickson. *A House in the City: A Guide to Buying and Renovating Old Rowhouses.* New York: Van Nostrand Reinhold Co., 1971.

Miller, Terry. *Greenwich Village and How It Got That Way.* New York: Crown Publishers, 1990.

Sawyers, Jane Skinner, ed. *The Greenwich Village Reader: Fiction, Poetry, and Reminiscences, 1872–2002.* New York: Cooper Square Press, 2001.

Schwarz, Judith. *Radical Feminists of Heterodoxy: Greenwich Village, 1912–1940.* Lebanon, NH: New Victoria Publishers, 1982.

Shapiro, Mary J. *Greenwich Village.* New York: Dover, 1985.

Sochen, June. *The New Woman: Feminism in Greenwich Village, 1910–1920.* New York: Quadrangle Books, 1972.

Stansell, Christine. *American Modern: Bohemian New York and the Creation of a New Century*. New York: Metropolitan Books, 2000.

Stern, Robert A. M. et al. *New York 1900*. New York: Rizzoli, 1983.

———. *New York 1930*. New York: Rizzoli, 1987.

———. *New York 1960*. 2nd Ed. New York: Monacelli, 1997.

Stokes, I. N. Phelps. *The Iconography of Manhattan Island, 1498–1909*. New York: Robert H. Dodd, 1915–28.

Trimberger, Ellen Kay. "Feminism, Men, and Modern Love: Greenwich Village, 1900–1925," in *Powers of Desire: The Politics of Sexuality*. Anne Snitow and Christine Stansell, and Sharon Thompson, eds. New York: Monthly Review Press, 1983.

Voorsanger, Catherine Hoover and John K. Howat, eds. *Art and the Empire City: New York, 1825–1861*. New Haven: Yale University Press, c. 2000.

Ware, Caroline F. *Greenwich Village, 1920–1930*. Boston: Houghton Mifflin, 1935.

Wertheim, Arthur Frank. *The New York Little Renaissance, 1908–1917*. New York: New York University Press, 1976.

Wetzsteon, Ross. *Republic of Dreams: Greenwich Village, the American Bohemia, 1910–1960*. New York: Simon & Schuster, c. 2002.

Zaleski, Jeffrey P. *The Greenwich Village Waterfront: An Historical Study*. New York: Greenwich Village Society for Historic Preservation, 1986.

Index

A

Adams, Abigail and John, 51
Aesthetic movement, 133
Age of Innocence, The (Wharton), 167
Alley house, 98, 99–100, *101–105*
Alley, Mr. and Mrs. Saul, 99, 100
Alphabet City, East Village, 183
A.M. Bininger & Co., 151
American Builder's Companion, The
 (Benjamin), 69
American City Beautiful move-
 ment, 20
American Museum of Folk Art, 197
antebellum period, 17, 63, 127
apartment buildings, 15, 21, 23, 51, 100,
 107, 108, 119, 130, 141, 211
architectural drawings, 25
"Artist in Japan, An" (Blum), 31
artists' colony, 15, 16, 21, 24, 32, 41, 59,
 88, 168, *170*, 183
artist studios, *150*, *151*, *152*, *153*
 of Blum house, 31, 32, 33–35
 of Dougdale, 60, 63, 65–67
 of Schary, 87, 88, 94, 97
 in Washington Square, 100
Art Students League, 87, 168
Astor, John Jacob, 51
Auden, W. H., 183
Avery, Humphrey Roger, 143

B

back houses, 32, 107, 159
Baird, Matthew, 193, 197
Banks, William, 31, 41
Barnes, Djuna, 15
Barrett, William, 88
Bayley Richards, Mary, 127
Beat Generation, 183
Beauties of Modern Architecture, The
 (Lafever), 81, 130
Benjamin, Asher, 69
Bininger, Abraham M., 151
Bininger, Isaac, 151
Bininger house, *150*, *151*, *152–57*

Blum, Robert, 31–32, 37
Blum house, *30*, 31–32, *33–40*
bohemian culture, 16, 21, 24, 32, 88, 159,
 168, 183
Boorman, James, 99
Boorman & Johnston, 99
Boston Art Club, 41
Bourne, Samuel E., 127
Bourne house, *126*, 127, *128*, *129*, 130,
 131–37
Brevoort Jr., Henry, 167
brewery industry, 175
Brewster, Joseph, 81
brick style homes, 51, 59, 69, 87, 98,
 106, 107, 116, 119, *126*, *138*, *158*, 175, *202*
British style, 19
Brown, David S., 70
brownstones, 16, 23, 51, 68, 139, 141, 151,
 167, 176
 See also Italianate style
Burr, Aaron, 51

C

Carrère & Hastings, 31
Chapin, Anna Alice, 176
Cherner, Ben, 183–84, 187
Cherner, Norman, 184, 187
Cherner, Thomas, 187
Cherner Chair, 184
Cherner Chair Company, 187
Cherner-O'Neill house, *182*, 183–84,
 184–91
Chicago Plan of 1907, 32
Chicago World's Columbian
 Exposition, 20
Christie house, *106*, 107, 107–8, *108–115*
Christopher Park, 14
Churches
 Church of St. John, *21*
 Church of the Ascension, 4, 6, 167
 Congregational Church, 176
 First Baptist Church, 176
 First Presbyterian, 167

Grace Church, 20
 Reformed Dutch Church, 19
 Trinity Church, 59, 60
cigar industry, 117
Classical style. *See* Neoclassical style
Classic New York (Huxtable), 51
Collegiate Gothic style, 19
Columbia University, 184
colonial houses, 59
Colonnade Row (La Grange
 Terrace), 19
Committee on Fine Arts of the State
 of New York, 41
Corinthian columns, 19, *173*
Corso, Gregory, 183
counterculture, 15, 16, 18, 21, 24, 32, 88,
 159, 183
Country Builder's Assistant, The
 (Benjamin), 69
Cummings, E. E., 15

D

Daily, Clifford Reed, 4
Daniel, Charles, 87
Davis & Dakin, 19
*Death and Life of Great American
 Cities, The* (Jacobs), 24
DeLancey, Susannah, 175
Depew, William, 69–70
Depew house, *68*, 69–70, *70–79*
diversity, 15, 21, 24, 51
Donlin, Edward J., 143
Doric columns, *68*, 69, *123*
Dos Passos, John, 159
Dougdale, John, 60, 63
Dreiser, Theodore, 159
Duveneck, Frank, 31

E

East Village, 15, 51, 183, 187
English style, 19
Erie Canal, 69–70, 108, 127

Editor: Andrea Danese
Designer: Ellen Nygaard
Production Manager: Jules Thomson

Library of Congress Cataloging-in-Publication Data

Murphy, Kevin D.
  The houses of Greenwich Village / Kevin D. Murphy ;
photography by Paul Rocheleau.
     p. cm.
Includes bibliographical references.
ISBN 978-0-8109-9520-8
  1. Architecture, Domestic—New York (State)—New York—19th century.
2. New York (N.Y.)—Buildings, structures, etc. 3. Greenwich Village
(New York, N.Y.)—Buildings, structures, etc. I. Rocheleau, Paul. II. Title.

NA735.N5M87 2008
728'.312097471—dc22
                          2007042042

Printed and bound in China
10 9 8 7 6 5 4 3 2 1

HNA
harry n. abrams, inc.
a subsidiary of La Martinière Groupe
Harry N. Abrams, Inc.
115 West 18th Street
New York, NY 10011
www.hnabooks.com